THE HATLESS MAN

THE HATLESS MAN

· · · · · · · · · · ·

An Anthology of
Odd & Forgotten Manners

SARAH KORTUM

DRAWINGS BY
RONALD SEARLE

VIKING

VIKING
Published by the Penguin Group
Penguin Books USA Inc., 375 Hudson Street, New York, New York 10014, U.S.A.
Penguin Books Ltd, 27 Wrights Lane, London W8 5TZ, England
Penguin Books Australia Ltd, Ringwood, Victoria, Australia
Penguin Books Canada Ltd, 10 Alcorn Avenue, Toronto, Ontario, Canada M4V 3B2
Penguin Books (N.Z.) Ltd, 182–190 Wairau Road, Auckland 10, New Zealand

Penguin Books Ltd, Registered Offices: Harmondsworth, Middlesex, England

First published in 1995 by Viking Penguin, a division of Penguin Books USA Inc.

1   3   5   7   9   10   8   6   4   2

Grateful acknowledgment is made for permission to reprint excerpts from the following copyrighted works:
Etiquette by Emily Post. Copyright 1922, 1942, 1950 by Funk & Wagnalls Company. By permission of HarperCollins Publishers.
Children Are People by Emily Post. Copyright 1940 by Funk & Wagnalls Company. By permission of HarperCollins Publishers.
Galateo Or *The Book of Manners* by Giovanni Della Casa, translated by R. S. Pine-Coffin (Penguin Classics, 1958).
Copyright © R. S. Pine-Coffin, 1958. By permission of Penguin Books Ltd.
Accent on Elegance by Geneviève Antoine Dariaux. Published by Doubleday & Company, Inc. Copyright © 1969, 1970 by
Geneviève Antoine Dariaux. By permission of the author.

LIBRARY OF CONGRESS CATALOGING-IN-PUBLICATION DATA
Kortum, Sarah.
The hatless man : an anthology of odd and forgotten manners / by Sarah Kortum : drawings by Ronald Searle.
p.   cm.
ISBN 0-670-86497-8
1. Etiquette—United States.   2. Etiquette—Great Britain.   I. Title.
BJ1854.K67   1995
395'.0973—dc20   95-9011

This Book Is Dedicated to

THE HATLESS MAN

Whose Photograph Was Found Hidden in a Copy of

THE BAZAR BOOK OF DECORUM

© 1870

Only the man whose hair stays put
should attempt to go hatless in town.
—AMY VANDERBILT

ACKNOWLEDGMENTS

For help in the procurement of books: Grateful thanks to the late Ed Mannion (for his indefatigable and quirky collecting), and Carolyn Perkins (for her generous loan to a complete stranger).

Additional thanks to: Barbara Bevan, Pamela Castillo, Anne Dinney, Jim Donato, Maxine Durney, Ruby Brown Eatherton, Ilona Granet, Chris Klingebiel and Lucy Kortum.

For help along the way: Dave Calver (for getting me started), Claudia Cohl (for broadening my vision), Major General John P. Condon, John Locke, Margaret Talcott, David Waldman and my agent, Phyllis Wender (for her loyalty and patience).

With love to Barry Maddock (for giving me the lighthouse), and my parents, Jean and Karl (for bestowing their love of the past, esteem for self-propelled endeavors, and faith in perseverance).

In warm memory of William R. Durney—who had the best manners of them all.

Contents

INTRODUCTION

I was handed my first book of etiquette at the age of thirty-one. I opened its pages expecting to look upon the dated counsel of the author with the amused superiority of having been born half a century later. The book was *Manners for Men*, its date 1897, its author Mrs. Humphry.

I shall always be grateful that it was Mrs. Humphry and not one of her drier colleagues, who introduced me to the world of etiquette. Instead of repelling me, the entertaining Mrs. Humphry hooked me, and soon I was burrowed in a musty library corner reading the first of what would eventually become over three hundred books read.

It wasn't the finger bowl rules that captivated me, the upper-class know-how, the sense of exclusiveness. It was the etiquette authors' vehemence, their urge to set the world straight. The image of the prissy, proper do-gooder authoress quickly vanished only one or two books into my reading. Many of the writers seemed to care less about the examples of good than of bad. And they weren't always so nice in their efforts to enlighten the populace. Just how courteous was the author who wrote: "If anything will sicken and disgust a man, it is the affected mincing way in which some people choose to talk. It is perfectly nauseous. If these young jackanapes who screw their words into all manner of diabolical shapes could only feel how perfectly disgusting they were, it might induce them to drop it."

Soon I was devouring the antiquated and animated language of etiquette past with the ease of magazine browsing at a supermarket checkout line. A feeling of fondness for the writers grew. As I opened their dust-covered tomes, I sensed that I was the first in many years to hear their muffled cries for order and propriety. Out of the pages fell pressed flowers, brittle photographs, self-improvement lists ("Admit ignorance Ask questions—people like questions sence when one has heard enough of you") and faded letters ("May 28, 1896, Dear Mother Gordon, Your kind note read and I was very glad to hear from you. I was sorry to hear that you have so sore a finger"). Could no hands other than my own have turned these pages in all of the twentieth century? Some of the books dated back to a time when pages had to be cut before being read, and, sadly, some of the pages had never been cut, but remained as fresh and virginal as the day they left the printing press.

With an etiquette book in hand I felt the exhilaration of time travel, for here was a chance to peek, close up, into the bedrooms and ballrooms of the past. Where else could one eavesdrop on the murmurs between butler and mistress, suitor and sweetheart, and know that these words were tried and true?

But the etiquette authors did not confine their advice to the parlor. They strayed out into the streets of their time. "When to Snub Reporters" was listed in the same table of contents as "Manners of Servants." "Harmony Between Husband and Wife" ("Never forget to be your wife's lover," reminds one book) and "Duties of a Wife" were considered as fitting topics in a book on manners as anniversary announcements.

It didn't take me long to realize that etiquette books were the self-help books of the past. They didn't just tell their readers how to eat and how to walk. They told them what books to read and what art to buy, how to develop full breasts and cure a pug nose, when to break up a romance (in November) and where (in front of a Titian or a Renoir at the National Gallery or the Tate), and even how to jump off a sinking steamboat (never "into the water in front of the paddle wheels while the wheels are in motion. . . . They should leap from behind the wheels if possible, when they find it necessary to take to the water"). Even the sheepishness that accompanies the desire for self-improvement was evident. Reports one etiquette author in 1869 about her genre of books: "People purchase them with an uneasy sense of shame, read them *sub rosa,* and keep them out of sight."

Scratch the surface of etiquette, and you will discover that it is not about bridesmaids and finger bowls but about how to become a better person in contact with others. Decorum cannot exist on a desert island; it requires the interaction of two. Yet behind the smallest of gestures—the offering of a chair, the opening of a door—is the greatest of principles. "All the various rules of etiquette for the government of society are but notes and commentaries on the one great rule, 'Love thy neighbor as thyself,' " explains an author. "The woman who refuses to move forward in a crowded [street] car, or occupies a seat and a half when the car is less crowded, does not love her neighbor . . ." observes another.

As trivial or arbitrary as the rules may seem, the true gentleman or lady would always adhere to them, for their allegiance was not to the rule but to the *omission of offense.* "You ought to remember that good manners consist precisely of annoying nobody," types an etiquette author in 1970. Four hundred years earlier a colleague penned a similar thought: "If everyone in town has short hair, it is wrong to grow long tresses, just as it is wrong to go clean-shaven if everyone else has a beard, because this implies contradiction of others, which is a thing never to be done except in case of necessity. . . ."

Of course, the fashions of right and wrong might change, and change they did, at an alarming rate. Instructs an author in 1886: "Ladies should be particular not to cross their knees in sitting, nor to assume any indecorous attitude." Fifty years later the fair miss was emancipated by the shifting decrees of decorum: "By all means, sit in any position you like, so long as you have pretty legs."

"Manners are growing very nearly as fickle as modes, and they date you as unmistakably. Last year's etiquette, in fact, may be this year's humor: just a quaint old custom," writes a woman in 1933. But these small details, these crossed or uncrossed legs, are neither insignificant nor unnoteworthy, for behind the minor gesture lies the major social trend. One writer intuitively sensed this when she observed in 1878: "Books that treat of men, and manners, and customs of the times, live longer than many nobler works dealing with less popular subjects. The reader of one hundred years hence may find even more interest in them (as revealing the characteristics of the society of their times), than do the present generation." One hundred and seventeen years later her words have become prophetic.

SARAH KORTUM
California, 1995

Chapter 1

MANNERS
FOR LOVERS
AND SPINSTERS
And Other Sweethearts

COURTING DAYS

"Accepting presents from gentlemen is a dangerous thing," warns an etiquette writer. A lady could receive a pretty basket of fruit, some sheet music, a box of confectionery, one or two autographs of distinguished persons, a riding whip or a pet dog, kitten, or bird (all being "trifles" and obligating no return should the relationship come to an end); but she must never accept a bracelet or brooch, nor even a hatpin or gloves (the latter, while less expensive, "being of a rather intimate sort").

If she found these categories too difficult to discern, then she had better abstain from gifts altogether and limit her gains to gardenias. Even flowers were not so innocent as first perceived, for they could be arranged to say the most scandalous things, reveal the etiquette writers. "Many a burning declaration of love has been made through their silent meanings," confides one author, who proceeds to list (as did many of her colleagues) the popular connotations for more than six hundred plants.

Thus the knowledgeable miss learned to be less delighted with a silken fan than with a bouquet of ivy (which symbolized "Fidelity, Marriage") interspersed with bay leaves ("No change til death"). She might answer a request for love with a handful of daisies, but a gentleman caller had better know his horticulture, for there was a subtle distinction between the message of a garden daisy ("I share your feelings") and that of a wild daisy ("I will think of it"). The courtship was on if either partner presented the other with a pineapple ("You are perfect"), but rocky if one arrived with broken corn ("quarrel"). The end was in sight (although the cook might be pleased) if a suitor arrived with a clump of basil ("hatred"). An astute young lady might respond with cactus ("Thou leavest me"), a handful of dead leaves ("sadness"), one deep red carnation ("Alas! for my poor heart"), and some hemlock ("You will cause my death"). If this collection failed to produce pity in the heart of the suitor, she might send a head of lettuce flying in his direction, which stated, unequivocally, that he was "cold-hearted."

"Presents should excite surprise and pleasure, therefore, you ought to involve them in a little mystery, and present them with an air of joyful kindness."

THE LADIES' HAND-BOOK OF ETIQUETTE
Anonymous, ca. 1867

"A present should be made with as little parade and ceremony as possible. If it is a small matter, a gold pencil-case, a thimble to a lady, or an affair of that sort, it should not be offered formally, but in an indirect way,—left in her basket, or slipped on to her finger, by means of a ribbon attached to it without a remark of any kind."

MANNERS, CULTURE AND DRESS OF THE BEST AMERICAN SOCIETY
Richard A. Wells, 1890

"Never present a gift saying that it is of no use to yourself."

HILL'S MANUAL OF SOCIAL AND BUSINESS FORMS
Thos. E. Hill, 1882

•   •   •

"People who open a gift package as imperturbably as they unpack their grocery bags are ill-mannered too."

ACCENT ON ELEGANCE
Geneviève Antoine Dariaux, 1970

"If you pay a lady a compliment, let it drop from your lips as if it were the accidental and unconscious expression of a profound truth."

THE STANDARD BOOK ON POLITENESS, GOOD BEHAVIOR AND
SOCIAL ETIQUETTE
Anonymous, 1884

"Do not be always undervaluing her rival in a woman's presence, nor mistaking a woman's daughter for her sister. These antiquated and exploded attempts denote a person who has learned the world more from books than men."

DECORUM
Anonymous, 1877

"Significant looks and gestures are equally objectionable, and must be avoided by all who desire to soar above positive vulgarity."

MARTINE'S HAND-BOOK OF ETIQUETTE
Arthur Martine, 1866

"Do be protective. Even independent modern girls like to be reassured about mice and spiders, rollercoasters and thunderstorms."

IF YOU PLEASE!
Betty Allen and Mitchell Pirie Briggs, 1942

"Lovers would do well to remember that hedges have ears as well as stone walls."

GEMS OF DEPORTMENT
Anonymous, 1880

"Clandestine courtships are the bane of families. They make fathers ill-tempered, brothers horse-whippish inclined, mothers nervous and ill, and the girls themselves generally the dupes of fortune-hunters."

ADVICE TO YOUNG LADIES *from* The London Journal *of 1855 and 1862*
Selected by R.D., 1933

"Any married woman may act as chaperon. 'Young and twenty' may chaperon 'fat and forty' if the former has the prefix 'Mrs.' before her name and the latter is still of the 'Miss' period."

EVERYDAY ETIQUETTE
Marion Harland and Virginia Van de Water, 1907

"Avoid, as a hostess or mother, making remarks about young people in the presence of others, such as 'one is only young once,' or coughing and rattling the door in a semi-humorous way, where young people are known to be sitting."

CAN I HELP YOU?
Viola Tree, 1937

"Avoid looking at a boy with your soul in your eyes."

MANNERS AND CONDUCT IN SCHOOL AND OUT
The Deans of Girls in Chicago High Schools, 1921

"No girl should permit a boy to be so familiar as to toy with her hands, or play with her rings; to handle her curls, or encircle her waist with his arm. Such impudent intimacy should never be tolerated for a moment."

GOOD MORALS AND GENTLE MANNERS
Alex M. Gow, 1873

•   •   •

"No girl should permit a boy to be so familiar as to toy with her hands, or play with her rings. . . . Such impudent intimacy should never be tolerated for a moment."

"[I]t is now held by many that the prudent and modest maiden should not even allow her lover, (even after their engagement), to kiss her. Not until after marriage should such a favor be granted."

MODERN MANNERS AND SOCIAL FORMS
Julia M. Bradley, 1889

"Wear a taffeta slip that *who-o-shes* and *crackles* when you move. This makes men delirious. . . . Rub your thighs together when you walk. The *squish-squish* sound of nylon also has a frenzying effect."

THE COSMO GIRL'S GUIDE TO THE NEW ETIQUETTE
Gael Greene and Jeannie Sakol, et al., 1971

"Don't flutter ecstatically around men, as if you were a moth and they were a light, and you wanted to get close but were afraid of singeing your wings. To most men this signifies that you have already been burned. . . . Besides, men don't like 'fluttering' women."

DON'TS FOR EVERYBODY
Compiled by Frederic Reddale, 1907

"Don't be continually talking about what a great beau you were in your younger days. That you are still unmarried is sufficient evidence that you were, at least, an unsuccessful one."

DON'TS FOR EVERYBODY
Compiled by Frederic Reddale, 1907

"Don't talk about your 'conquests.' It sounds silly. Leave it to silly girls. Silliness is excusable in young girls, but not in old maids."

DON'TS FOR EVERYBODY
Compiled by Frederic Reddale, 1907

POPPING THE QUESTION

A gentleman should never lose his dignity when proposing to a woman. If there was any chance that he was "likely to break down, or is not prepared to take a refusal gracefully . . . he had far better entrust his cause to his pen," urges an etiquette writer.

But it was best to propose in person, no matter how garbled the practiced speech came out. "Never lose an opportunity," insists one author. "Women cannot make direct advances, but they use infinite tact in giving men occasions to make them." If she had maneuvered him out to the gazebo, the panicked suitor had no choice "though he may tremble, and feel his pulses throbbing and tingling through every limb; though his heart is filling up his throat, and his tongue cleaves to the roof of his mouth, yet the awful question must be asked. . . ."

As expected as the proposal was, the maiden was not to blurt out an immediate "Yes!" but was to hesitate in a little pantomime of "real or feigned embarrassment," coached one book, accompanied by a bit of surprise.

Women were not to view their refusals of marriage as matters of triumph, nor were men to exhibit sudden switches of personality. "Rejected suitors sometimes act as if they had received injuries they were bound to avenge, and so take every opportunity of annoying or slighting the helpless victims of their former attentions," describes an author. "Such conduct is cowardly and unmanly, to say nothing of its utter violation of good breeding."

"To keep a lady's company six months is a public announcement of an engagement."

SEARCH LIGHTS ON HEALTH
Prof. B. G. Jefferis and J. L. Nichols, 1896

"A gentleman should never propose to a lady who is a guest at his own home."

MODERN MANNERS AND SOCIAL FORMS
Julia M. Bradley, 1889

"A beautiful head of hair is no insignificant item in a girl's dowry."

MODERN MANNERS AND SOCIAL FORMS
Julia M. Bradley, 1889

"Don't marry the woman who reads novels, and dreams of being a duchess or a countess, or the wife of a multi-millionaire."

DON'TS FOR EVERYBODY
Compiled by Frederic Reddale, 1907

"Don't marry any female who is too young—(say fifteen.) Nor any woman who has a red nose, at any age; because people make observations as you go along the street."

THE AMERICAN CHESTERFIELD
Lord Chesterfield, 18—

"A timid woman should never marry a hesitating man, lest, like frightened children, each keep perpetually re-alarming the other by imaginary fears."

SEARCH LIGHTS ON HEALTH
Prof. B. G. Jefferis and J. L. Nichols, 1896

"Don't marry a man who has no time for dogs. Ten to one such a man will only have time for himself."

THINGS THAT ARE NOT DONE
Edgar and Diana Woods, 1937

"If you would have a serene old age never woo a girl who keeps a diary."

THE CYNIC'S RULES OF CONDUCT
Chester Field, Jr., 1905

"A gentleman should never lose his dignity when proposing to a woman. If there was any chance that he was likely to break down, or is not prepared to take a refusal gracefully . . . he had far better entrust his cause to his pen."

TYING THE KNOT

A bride's trousseau was expected to include: One wedding gown, a veil, one tailor gown and jacket, one visiting gown, one reception gown, one dinner gown, one silk party gown, one house gown, one negligee, one bathrobe, two short dressing jackets in silk or flannel, four sets of underwear, including one bridal set, two fancy silk waists, two silk shirts, four pairs of silk stockings, six pairs of cotton stockings, one dozen handkerchiefs, one pair of heavy kid boots, one pair of evening slippers, one pair of house shoes, six pairs of gloves, one handsome hat, one plain hat, one long plain coat, one handsome wrap, one short jacket, and one evening wrap.

With such an elaborate sewing deadline before her, it was no surprise that many a bride wore "herself to shreds in the effort to get her new clothing made. I have seen brides so worn, so pale, so 'tuckered out' by the sewing of weary weeks, that they went like wan ghosts to the altar; they had used up nervous tissue so shamefully that they were unfit to enter on marriage," describes an author.

But intricate finery, after weeks of arduous needlework, could come to nothing if worn poorly, for the demeanor of the bride was paramount. "She is no longer expected to advance up the aisle at a funereal pace, as though she were going to an execution," advised one turn-of-the-century author. This paid a poor compliment to the insecure groom, standing nervously at the altar. Nor was she to snivel and sniff as she advanced. "Crying is no longer fashionable. It has followed fainting into the moonlight land of half-forgotten things," continues the author. "The bride of to-day is brisk and bright. She recognises the golden rule of good manners as it obtains at present to ignore all that is sad and serious in life, its sounding depths, its coral reefs, and to playfully sport in the shallows, while mingling with one's world."

"A very young lady should have bridesmaids of her own age, but a bride who is no longer in her girlhood should choose bridesmaids who will not make her look old and ugly by comparison."

GOOD MANNERS

Anonymous, 1870

"The skirt should have a train varying in length with the fashion, but never so long as to interfere with the bride's movements. Several yards of satin trailing upon the floor will result in pulling her head back at every step, producing a very awkward and ugly effect."

GOOD FORM FOR ALL OCCASIONS

Florence Howe Hall, 1914

"Congratulations are sometimes too fervidly put. When, for instance, the bride is a little past the bloom of youth and brightness, it is well for her friends and acquaintances not to be too gushingly insistent with their congratulations. To be so is rather to suggest that she has been successful against terrible odds."

MANNERS FOR GIRLS

Mrs. Humphry, 1901

"The dress worn by a guest at a wedding may be as rich as desired, but should not have a bridal appearance. Sometimes a recent bride wears her own wedding gown at a friend's wedding; but it is in better taste not to do so, nor in any other way to invite comparisons."

ETIQUETTE

Agnes H. Morton, 1892

"It is not the correct thing for enthusiastic friends to throw old shoes with such force as to break the carriage windows or frighten the horses."

THE CORRECT THING IN GOOD SOCIETY

Florence Howe Hall, 1902

TILL DEATH DO US PART

"The beginnings of married life are so important as to be solemn," declares one etiquette writer. Solemnity might quickly turn into hysteria and panic if a timid young maiden was pursued by an aggressive groom. "Usually marriage is consummated within a day or two after the ceremony, but this is gross injustice to the bride," cautions one book. "In most cases she is nervous, timid, and exhausted by the duties of preparation for the wedding, and in no way in a condition, either in body or mind, for the vital change which the married relation bring upon her."

To plunge ahead insensitively was perhaps to render an unhealthy wife, and no man would wish to risk that. "If the queen of his castle sits in the darkness of dyspepsia, or writhes in the agonies of ticdouloureux, the recollection that she shone as the bright particular star at Madame Pompadour's finishing seminary, or that at Saratoga last season she astonished even the professionals with her execution of Bach's compositions, will not penetrate the gloom of his home with a single ray of light. His house may be filled with servants, but only one being is near and dear to him, and that one petulantly whines, 'O, don't light the gas, I can't bear the light; and please don't walk so heavy. O Charles, please don't speak so loud! O dear me, my head is dreadful! O dear me, dear me!' "

To circumvent this possibility in the first days of marriage "[y]oung husbands should wait for an *invitation to the banquet,* and they will be amply paid by the very pleasure sought," instructs one book. "To be sure, there are some women who are possessed of more forward natures and stronger desires than others. In such cases there may be less trouble."

"Neither partner should take along a pet on the honeymoon. Pets can be jealous creatures—and provoke jealousy."

AMY VANDERBILT'S ETIQUETTE
Amy Vanderbilt, 1972

•   •   •

"[T]here are some women who are possessed of
more forward natures and stronger desires than others."

"As a husband, share your knowledge of the activities of life with your wife, who, from the very nature of her occupation is excluded from much of its exciting whirl. Read together, talk together of art, of music, of literature, of the stirring events of the outer world, and put afar the evil day when topics of mutual interest shall have been worn so threadbare that the average man and woman must feel a strange desire to fall asleep directly dinner is over."

SOCIAL ETIQUETTE
Maud C. Cooke, 18—

"We know a lovely lady of complete leisure who provided always the same small square cheese cracker for her husband's excellent cocktails, though he rushed home from the office, got into evening clothes, and mixed the drinks. She lost him eventually. We always knew she would, though all appeared serene. Mental inertia and lack of imagination is just as fatal in serving food as in any other activity."

CASUAL MEALS
Anne Pierce, 1936

"Never address a person by his or her initial letter, as 'Mr. C.,' or 'Mr. S.' It is as vulgar as a fishmonger's style. What can be more abominable than to hear a woman speak of her husband as 'Mr. P.!' as though he had become whittled down, in her estimation, until there is nothing left of him but a single letter."

THE LADY'S BOOK OF MANNERS
Anonymous, 1870

"If a woman . . . has had more than four husbands, she poisons them,— avoid her."

THE AMERICAN CHESTERFIELD
Lord Chesterfield, 18—

Chapter 2

MANNERS
FOR BUTLERS
AND SCULLERY MAIDS
And Other Servants

UPSTAIRS, DOWNSTAIRS

Servants were expected to be in by half past ten, but the master and mistress of the house could dance until dawn and then arrive home fully expecting their personal attendants to be up and waiting. "Why servants should be expected to be able to do with less sleep than their employers is an idea that passes my comprehension," grumbles one writer, "more particularly as the former are probably passing the midnight hours in enjoying themselves, which is a very different matter from waiting hour after hour, till every muscle is aching with cold, for the return of the revellers."

At the first sounds of arrival, the lady's maid must be ready with a cup of hot cocoa to greet her mistress. If the master was suffering from too much port, the valet may be the man to carry his lordship up the stairs and even sit up the night with him (or sleep in his room), dispelling any phantoms that might arise. Meanwhile, the lady of the house was not to succumb to the temptation of confiding in the girl brushing her hair, unbuttoning her gown, and readying the bath that had been filled after numerous trips up and down the stairs with pails of hot water. No matter how exciting the evening's flirtation had been, she must never forget: "Familiarity with servants always arouses their contempt. . . ."

By 1924 all temptation was removed, for this scenario was declared obsolete. "The days when mistresses expected their maids to sit up for them at night are past," announces an etiquette author. "[S]urely women are not so helpless that they cannot take off their own clothes at night. It is degrading for people of average intelligence to allow themselves to sink into a state of dependence upon another individual to that extent."

"Haughty butlers are as much outmoded as snuff."

THE NEW ETIQUETTE
Margery Wilson, 1940

"It is not the correct thing to hire an English butler, and copy his drawl, imagining that you will thus learn to speak like a cultivated Englishman."

THE CORRECT THING IN GOOD SOCIETY
Florence Howe Hall, 1902

"A good butler knows everything, from the antecedents of the guests to the time-tables of the most suburban railways. He is very apt to have a fine taste in the arrangement of flowers, and the weather probabilities are seldom hid from him."

VOGUE'S BOOK OF ETIQUETTE
The Editors of Vogue, *1923*

"A butler is not permitted to wear a boutonnière, a white waistcoat, a satin-faced coat, patent leather shoes, or perfume. He must not flourish a colored handkerchief, nor wear rings or a watch chain. His watch he can slip, without fob or chain, into his waistcoat pocket; and the tie worn with his morning livery should be black or of a very subdued color and innocent of a pin."

ENCYCLOPAEDIA OF ETIQUETTE
Emily Holt, 1901

"No maid should ever be permitted to shuffle
around the house in bedroom slippers."

"[I]t is unnecessary to add that none but vulgarians would employ a butler (or any other house servant) who wears a mustache!"

ETIQUETTE
Emily Post, 1922

"A good servant is never awkward. His boots never creak; he never breathes hard, has a cold, is obliged to cough, treads on a lady's dress, or breaks a dish."

GOOD MANNERS
Anonymous, 1870

"Maids are supposed to *be* jewels, not to *wear* them."

THE BOOK OF GOOD MANNERS
Frederick H. Martens, 1923

"Don't expect the maid who does general housework to appear always as neatly attired and as agreeable to look upon as the dainty creature that trips across the stage with dust brush in hand in the modern comedy."

CORRECT SOCIAL USAGE, vol. I
Mrs. Harriet Hubbard Ayer, et al., 1906

"No maid should ever be permitted to shuffle around the house in bedroom slippers."

MAIDCRAFT
Lita Price and Harriet Bonnet, 1937

THE DUMB WAITER

In elegant households dinner was announced by the butler stealthily entering the drawing room, catching the eye of his mistress, and silently bowing. "To ring a bell to announce that dinner is ready is not good form," directs an author.

Bells were also taboo on top of the table, but foot-bells were allowed on the floor for hostesses to summon in servants from the kitchen without noise.

The correct ratio of servants to guests was a point of contention. One book suggested one servant for every two persons, while another advised one per six diners. Whatever the number, a guest's food must never be allowed to grow cold and unappetizing while a stingy staff of servants distributed the victuals at the far end of the room.

There could be as many as twenty-five servants for a dinner of fifty, but this formidable group was to recede into the woodwork during the course of the meal. Some families grew so accustomed to the presence of servants during mealtime that the help became invisible. This was careless, scolds one author: "To discuss private affairs or current gossip of an unkind nature, or to pass friends and acquaintances in critical review before servants is a serious mistake too often made in otherwise well-bred families."

A diner should not acknowledge the servants beyond a murmured "thank you" and certainly must *never* seek a reaction from them that was unforthcoming from his peers: "If you make any general remark, do not look up at the waiters to see what effect it has upon them," orders a writer. "If they are well-trained they will not move a muscle at hearing the most laughable story, nor will they give any sign whatever that they have not closed their ears like deaf adders to all that has been going on."

"If you ask the waiter for anything, you will be careful to speak to him gently in the tone of *request,* and not of *command*. To speak to a waiter in a driving manner will create, among well-bred people, the suspicion that you were sometime a servant yourself, and are putting on *airs* at the thought of your promotion."

THE PERFECT GENTLEMAN
By a Gentleman, 1860

•   •   •

"Never apologize to a waiter for requiring him to wait upon you; that is his business."

THE LADIES' AND GENTLEMEN'S ETIQUETTE
Mrs. E. B. Duffey, 1877

"Never, under any circumstances, no matter where you are, cry out 'Waiter!' No man of any breeding ever does it. Wait till you can catch the attendant's eye, and by a nod bring him to you."

THE MENTOR
Alfred Ayres, 1894

"Nothing is more inelegant than for the servants to carry piles of plates in their hands and distribute them about the table as though dealing cards."

THE BOOK OF GOOD MANNERS
Mrs. Burton Kingsland, 1901

"Many a mistress has died of nervous prostration brought on by the violent palpitation and nervous excitement caused by constantly seeing her new servant try how high a pyramid of plates she can carry in one hand, while she is tilting an irregular pile of cups and saucers in the other. When she slips and they go down, as much injury has been done to the poor mistress' constitution and as many nails have been knocked in her coffin as if she had lived to the age of Methuselah in that horrible five minutes."

THE HEARTHSTONE; OR, LIFE AT HOME
Laura C. Holloway, 1893

"The hostess who is launching commands, frowning, winking, and beckoning at her stupid servant throughout dinner has blundered beyond forgiveness."

CORRECT SOCIAL USAGE, vol. II
Margaret Watts Livingston, et al., 1906

•   •   •

"The mistress of the house, in short, should be to a cook what a publisher is to his authors—that is to say, competent to form a judgment upon their works, though himself incapable of writing even a magazine article."

COLLIER'S CYCLOPEDIA OF COMMERCIAL AND SOCIAL INFORMATION
Compiled by Nugent Robinson, 1882

Chapter 3

MANNERS
FOR GLUTTONS
AND GASTRONOMES
And Other Diners

A FEAST FOR EYES

That little square of cloth, commonly called the table napkin, could sink a hostess as surely as a diner, particularly if used to decorate a place setting.

As impressive as the fabric sculpture of boots, swans, ships, Alpine peaks, or bunny rabbits may be, "that is 'hotel style,' " frowns an author, and thus not at all elegant. It was offensive for more than aesthetic reasons, agrees a colleague: It "is a dirty fashion, requiring the manipulation of hands which are not always fresh, and as the napkin must be damp at the folding, it is not always dry when shaken out. Nothing is so unhealthy as a damp napkin; it causes agony to a delicate and nervous lady, a man with the rose-cold, a person with neuralgia or rheumatism, and is offensive to every one."

But once unfolded, the former bunny rabbit could betray the bungling diner as well. Don't panic, instruct the etiquette experts: "A person unaccustomed to the use of a table napkin, can learn the whole minutiae of handling it in twenty minutes."

Unfortunately, this education could quickly be brought to a halt if the napkin slithered right to the floor, the plight of many women with silken laps. "If such accidents *should* happen, pass them over slightly, and do not lose your temper," advises one author. "[K]eep always a pincushion in your pocket," she continues, and when no one is looking, fasten the napkin to your lap.

But once the cloth was brought out of hiding, please remember: "It is a towel, for wiping the lips and fingers in emergencies, but should be used un-obtrusively—not flourished like a flag of truce."

Finally, do not be seen, at dinner's end, struggling to refold the napkin back into its original shape, for "that would be an assumption on the part of the guest that the hostess would use it again before laundering," observes a writer. Simply drop the napkin *as is* onto the table, rise, and depart.

"When you sit down at table, it is not necessary to whisk the napkin gayly about before unfolding it. The concealed roll is certain to fly a considerable distance before alighting, and may even crack the enameling on one of the great ladies at the banquet."

MANNERS FOR THE METROPOLIS
Francis W. Crowninshield, 1909

"Very little starch should be put in napkins. No one wishes to wipe a delicate lip on a board, and a stiff napkin is very like that commodity."

MANNERS AND SOCIAL USAGES
Mrs. John Sherwood, 1897

"Men who wear a mustache are permitted to 'saw' the mouth with the napkin, as if it were a bearing-rein, but for ladies this would look too masculine."

MANNERS AND SOCIAL USAGES
Mrs. John Sherwood, 1897

"Gloves and veil may be removed before going to the table or the veil may merely be turned up at the table. A veil must never, of course, be allowed to hang so that each mouthful of food must be passed under the veil."

THE BOOK OF GOOD MANNERS
Victor H. Diescher, 1923

"The women remove their gloves and lay them in their laps. The habit of tucking them in at the wrists, or, worse, placing them in a wineglass, is inelegant."

THE BOOK OF GOOD MANNERS
Mrs. Burton Kingsland, 1901

"The table should be firm and solid, and not so shaky that the guests fear some catastrophe."

TWENTIETH CENTURY ETIQUETTE
Annie Randall White, 1900

"Never put your feet so far under the table as to touch those of the person on the opposite side; neither should you curl them under nor at the side of your chair."

HILL'S MANUAL OF SOCIAL AND BUSINESS FORMS
Thos. E. Hill, 1882

"Candles are very pretty, but exceedingly troublesome. The wind blows the flame to and fro; the insects flutter into the light; an unhappy moth seats himself on the wick, and burning into an unsightly cadaver makes a gutter down one side; the little red-paper shades take fire, and there is a general conflagration."

MANNERS AND SOCIAL USAGES
Mrs. John Sherwood, 1897

"There is one thing that should always be remembered by those who are arranging flowers for living-rooms—but more especially for a dinner-table—which is, never to make use of strong scented flowers. . . . One of the loveliest dinner-tables ever seen was composed of a large bed of lycopodium, arranged with stephanotis and lily-of-the-valley; but several of the party grew momentarily whiter and whiter, were unable to eat a morsel, and, in short, passed an evening of undeniable suffering, which no host or hostess would willingly inflict on their guests."

THE MANNERS OF THE ARISTOCRACY
By One of Themselves, 18—

"[I]t cannot be too strongly insisted upon that the ornaments—be they plants, *épergnes,* or fountains—should not be of such a height as to intervene between the faces of those who sit opposite each other. . . . [T]he diner-out has learned to dread the sight of a plant in a pot, which probably, according to the well-known contrariety of things, hides from him the very face that he would like best to look at. An occasional glimpse of the lady's nose, chin, or ear, through a leafy screen, however beautiful in itself, is too tantalising an occupation to be calculated to promote digestion."

THE MANNERS OF THE ARISTOCRACY
By One of Themselves, 18—

"Never have flowers floating—not even orchids. Flowers drown as quickly as people and look desolate like so many Ophelias."

CAN I HELP YOU?
Viola Tree, 1937

THE GOOD CARVER

To be well versed in "the art and mystery of cutting up" was one of the requirements of a gentleman, just as important as knowing how to fence, box, ride, row, shoot, skate, dance, and play at billiards. "Awkwardness in small things suggests awkwardness in great ones . . ." and so licensed, many etiquette book authors delved with great enthusiasm into the minutiae of cutting up goose and quail. It was painful for guests to see a man hacking for half an hour across bone, complains Lord Chesterfield, greasing himself and bespattering the company. "What more pitiable object can be imagined than a near-sighted individual struggling in the dissection of a pair of fowls of whose anatomy he is as ignorant as he is of that of a pterodactyl?" agrees a colleague. If you don't know how to carve, don't descend into a diatribe about the age of the fowl and the toughness of the meat. Confess your shortcomings and hand the knife over to the servant.

*"Never put your feet so far under the table as to
touch those of the person on the opposite side . . ."*

"Remember it is very vulgar to stand up to carve."

THE LADY'S BOOK OF MANNERS
Anonymous, 1870

"We must all at some time have had our appetite destroyed by the mangling process carried on by our host on an unfortunate fowl, in defiance of every law of anatomy or even common sense. We have often felt thankful, when receiving some nondescript piece, *haggled* off, and triumphantly presented, as though the carver were proud of his successful effort of detaching some portion, no matter in what condition, that the bird had been subjected to the process of fire, lest it should have flown at its torturer, and picked out his eyes in revenge."

MANNERS; OR HAPPY HOMES AND GOOD SOCIETY
Mrs. Hale, 1867

"When the host is carving, family and guests should forget him. If he is in trouble, it will not help to give him the hypnotic eye."

THE AIR FORCE WIFE
Nancy Shea; revised by Anna Perle Smith, 1966

IN ORDER OF COURSE

Symmetry was an important though subtle presence at a meal. "All the table paraphernalia should be placed with mathematical regularity," insists an authority. Even the food was to succumb to a greater order, arranged so that "each guest may remove a part easily and without destroying the symmetry of the whole." The platter was not to look "as devastated as a battlefield" after only two or three guests had helped themselves. But flowers were not to be called into service to maintain the balance. "Flowers should never be used to decorate dishes containing food," sniffs an author, as blundered one nouveau riche who shamefully "adorned her meat-platters with expensive roses, the stems disappearing in the gravy!"

"Never watch the dishes as they are uncovered, or cry out when you perceive something dainty."

COLLIER'S CYCLOPEDIA OF COMMERCIAL AND SOCIAL INFORMATION
Compiled by Nugent Robinson, 1882

"Don't, when offered a dish at a friend's table, look at it critically, turn it about with the spoon and fork, and then refuse it."

ETIQUETTE FOR WOMEN
G. R. M. Devereux, 1902

"Never use an eye-glass, either to look at the persons around you or the articles upon the table."

THE LADIES' BOOK OF ETIQUETTE, AND MANUAL OF POLITENESS
Florence Hartley, 1873

"Anything like greediness or indecision must not be indulged in. You must not take up one piece and lay it down in favor of another, or hesitate. It looks *gauche* in the extreme not to know one's mind about trifles."

SENSIBLE ETIQUETTE OF THE BEST SOCIETY
Compiled by Mrs. H. O. Ward, 1878

"In refusing to be helped to any particular thing, never give as a reason that 'you are afraid of it' . . . "

MISS LESLIE'S BEHAVIOUR BOOK
Miss Leslie, 1859

THE SILVER SPOON

"It's possible for your business prospects to be blighted or your whole social standing to be altered by a slip between the cup and the lip," warns one writer, for the table—more than any other place—was the barometer of true breeding. "A man may pass muster by dressing well, and may sustain himself tolerably in conversation; but if he be not perfectly *'au fait,'* dinner will betray him."

The well-bred diner knew to keep his knife—with its untidy associations—out of frequent view, although "the crusade against the knife should not be pushed too far," cautions one writer. Surely a knife could occasionally be seen to cut the food upon the plate or even to assist morsels gently onto the fork, "but there is no need of its being thrust into the mouths and throats of civilized people as if they were professional knife-swallowers."

A dinner knife is not a dagger, and any posture that reinforced this well-armed image was in poor taste. "The knife and fork should never be held vertically as if they were weapons," declares a writer; particularly "upright on each side of your plate while you are talking," adds another.

Scintillating conversation was no excuse for an abstracted diner pausing, loaded utensil midair, while he chased a few delectable tidbits of thought. Conversation must never interfere with the transport of food, insists a writer: "When he once starts towards his mouth with food, nothing should stop him from getting it in."

Nor should a diner hunch down to hasten the entry of victuals. "You bring it up to your erect head; you don't duck down to meet it coming up," remarks a colleague. "You shouldn't meet your food even halfway."

Correct utensil wielding is an art, proclaims another. To watch a diner load a fork with rice without spilling a kernel was "an added attraction to the dinner," she applauds. Why, a "deft-handed diner-out will acquire such skill in using the fork that his operations with it, like those of the professional pen-man with his pen, seem to exhibit something of artistic genius."

"Don't make a wall around your plate with your left arm, as if you feared somebody were going to snatch it from you."

ETIQUETTE FOR MODERNS
Gloria Goddard, 1941

•   •   •

"In refusing to be helped to any particular thing,
never give as a reason that 'you are afraid of it' . . ."

"Never hitch up your sleeves, as some men have the habit of doing, as though you were going to make mud pies."

THE MENTOR
Alfred Ayres, 1894

"Never carry your food to your mouth with any curves or flourishes, unless you want to look as though you were airing your company manners."

THE MENTOR
Alfred Ayres, 1894

"The soup is the stumbling-block for many people. Perform silently and don't sway your body rhythmically as the spoon is raised and lowered."

THINGS THAT ARE NOT DONE
Edgar and Diana Woods, 1937

"A brimming spoon implies, for any but the phenomenally steady hand, a chapter of awkward accidents."

THE CYCLOPAEDIA OF SOCIAL USAGE
Helen L. Roberts, 1913

"Never turn the spoon over and look at yourself in the bowl; it is the action of a clown."

AS OTHERS SEE US
Anonymous, 1890

"It is not the correct thing to put the spoon or fork so far into the mouth that the bystanders are doubtful of its return to the light."

THE CORRECT THING IN GOOD SOCIETY
Florence Howe Hall, 1902

"To overload the fork, and then with a sudden toss to throw its cargo into the mouth, is uncouth, and savors of the cheap restaurant style. Coolness and deliberation are essentials of graceful eating. Again, the fork should not be carried around until it stands at right angles to the mouth, and then be thrust vigorously in, as you would thrust a sword into an adversary's body."

MODERN MANNERS AND SOCIAL FORMS
Julia M. Bradley, 1889

"Never use your knife to convey your food from your plate to your mouth; besides being decidedly vulgar, you run the imminent danger of enlarging the aperture from ear to ear—by no means an obvious improvement on the female countenance. A lady of fashion used to say that she never saw a person guilty of this ugly habit without a shudder, as every minute she expected to see the head of the unfortunate severed from the body."

ETIQUETTE FOR THE LADIES
Anonymous, 1849

"To see a guest eat with his knife, and thrust it into his mouth, will send the cold chills up and down the spine of many hostesses."

MODERN MANNERS AND SOCIAL FORMS
Julia M. Bradley, 1889

"The changes of plates are kaleidoscopic. You take your soup in Sevres, your entrées in England, or Dresden, and so on, till you come to fruit in China or Japan. It is quite *en règle,* in these aesthetic times, to turn your plate over, with the sapient air of a connoisseur, and study the marks thereon inscribed. But it is well to avoid the catastrophe which befel an absent-minded man, who, forgetful that he had been helped, reversed his plate, and bestowed one of Delmonico's *bouchées à la reine* upon his neighbor's satin petticoat."

THE SUCCESSFUL HOUSEKEEPER
Anonymous, 1882

•   •   •

"It is not the correct thing to turn up the glass or mug on the nose, or to look
at people while drinking, either over or through the glass."

THE CORRECT THING IN GOOD SOCIETY
Florence Howe Hall, 1902

BON APPÉTIT

"[N]either etiquette nor heroism exact so great a sacrifice as that of swallow-
ing anything that offers a real danger," concedes an author. Should a guest be
forced by "a tactless entertainer" to give reason for refraining from a serving
of dubious mushrooms, it is not the time for uncompromising frankness. Far
better to say, "I am really obliged to practise abstinence in some of the courses
if I am to do justice to other temptations to follow."

But once in, etiquette authorities concur, by and large you must swallow,
as did one "gallant elderly bachelor who bravely swallowed a hairy caterpillar
with his lettuce leaf when he caught the agonized glance of his hostess, rather
than embarrass her." If you really feared for your life, there were nuances to
the removal of food. In 1663 one was allowed to throw "dext'rously forth
upon the ground" something that caused irksomeness, "taking it decently with
two fingers, or with the left hand half shut, so that it be not a liquid thing, in
such case one may more freely spit it on the ground, turning ones self if it be
possible somewhat aside. . . ." By 1972 Amy Vanderbilt wouldn't hear of such
behavior. You were to return the partly masticated morsel to your plate, she
insists, but camouflage it behind a wall of celery leaves or hide it under some
bread.

However stubborn the foreign body on your tongue "never use your napkin as a screen for your mouth as you grapple with the enemy." If you found
yourself losing the battle and convulsing in a fit of choking, help was on the
way if you were dining at the White House. Its cookbook claimed in 1890 that
a piece of food, lodged in the throat, could "sometimes be pushed down with
the finger, or removed with a hair-pin quickly straightened and hooked at the
end. . . ."

"*Although asparagus may be taken in the fingers, don't take a long drooping stalk, hold it up in the air and catch the end of it in your mouth like a fish.*"

"If on a diet, do not, as I have known an ill-bred person to do, expatiate on it and its good effects. I knew a man who always carried a certain bread with him proclaiming at every dinner table that he could eat no other."

GOOD MANNERS FOR ALL OCCASIONS
Margaret E. Sangster, 1921

"In dealing with bread, use neither knife nor fork. It must be broken with the fingers. There is a story of an absent-minded and short-sighted prelate who, with the remark, 'My bread, I think?' dug his fork into the white hand of a lady who sat beside him. He had been badly brought up, or he would not have used his fork, and the white hand would have experienced nothing worse than a sudden grasp."

MANNERS FOR MEN
Mrs. Humphry, 1897

"To take up a whole piece of bread or toast and leave the dentist's model of a bite in it seems uncouth. . . . Let us break our bread and nibble mouselike at the edge."

VOGUE'S BOOK OF ETIQUETTE
The Editors of Vogue, *1923*

"Strong people may eat cucumbers in small quantities, but it is a severe trial to a weak stomach, and is far from a good thing for even the best stomach. I quite agree with the celebrated Dr. Abernethy, who gives the following directions for preparing a cucumber: 'Peel it, slice it down into thin pieces, put vinegar and pepper to it, and then throw it away.' "

FIVE-MINUTE CHATS WITH YOUNG WOMEN, AND CERTAIN OTHER PARTIES
Dio Lewis, 1874

"Lord and Lady B——, names familiar some years back to the students of the 'high-life' columns of our papers, were at a dinner-party in New York with an acquaintance of mine who painted the scene for me. Lady B——, tasting her soup as soon as it was set down in front of her, calls to her husband at the other end of the table: 'B———, my dear! Don't eat this soup! It is *quite filthy!* There are tomatoes in it!' "

EVERYDAY ETIQUETTE
Marion Harland and Virginia Van de Water, 1907

"If a dish is distasteful to you, decline it, but make no remarks about it. It is sickening and disgusting to explain at a table how one article makes you sick, or why some other dish has become distasteful to you. I have seen a well-dressed tempting dish go from a table untouched, because one of the company told a most disgusting anecdote about finding vermin served in a similar dish."

MARTINE'S HAND-BOOK OF ETIQUETTE
Arthur Martine, 1866

"Still less say of anything which you enjoy at table, 'I love it.' 'I love melons,' 'I love peaches,' 'I adore grapes'—these are school-girl utterances. We love our friends. Love is an emotion of the heart, but not one of the palate. We like, we appreciate grapes, but we do not love them."

THE AMERICAN CODE OF MANNERS
Anonymous, 1880

"Do not praise bad wine, for it will persuade those who are judges that you are an ignoramus or a flatterer."

THE PERFECT GENTLEMAN
By a Gentleman, 1860

"It is not elegant to *gnaw* Indian corn. The kernals should be scored with a knife, scraped off into the plate, and then eaten with a fork. Ladies should be particularly careful how *they* manage so ticklish a dainty, lest the exhibition rub off a little desirable romance."

HINTS ON ETIQUETTE
Charles William Day, 1843

"Although asparagus may be taken in the fingers, don't take a long drooping stalk, hold it up in the air and catch the end of it in your mouth like a fish."

ETIQUETTE
Emily Post, 1922

"Idiots swallow oysters. Epicures bite them, as if they were chicken."

CAN I HELP YOU?
Viola Tree, 1937

"A ring of fruit stones, all around the edge of the plate, stamps you as being an outsider. It is a small thing; but just collect the stones in an irregular heap."

THINGS THAT ARE NOT DONE
Edgar and Diana Woods, 1937

"Never demonstrate your physical strength by crushing a walnut in your fist or in the crook of your arm—never in a restaurant, at least."

ACCENT ON ELEGANCE
Geneviève Antoine Dariaux, 1970

"Cast not thy bones vnder the Table."

THE BOKE OF NURTURE, OR SCHOOLE OF GOOD MANNERS
Compyled by Hugh Rhodes, 1577

"[I]t is reminiscent of boarding-school days and positively barbaric to bite, poke, squeeze, or break candies to investigate the filling and then put them back in the box."

THE ARMY WIFE
Nancy Shea; revised by Anna Perle Smith, 1966

FOOD FOR THOUGHT

The obituary for John Andrew Malkeith listed his occupation as "*quatorzième,* or fourteenth man at table." Never, urged the etiquette books, *never* have thirteen at a dinner party. There was a superstition, possibly dating back to the Last Supper, that should thirteen gather round a dinner table one would die in the year to come. If a guest should fail to arrive, let the host graciously bow out of the group lest the assemblage drop to thirteen.

Malkeith, who died at the age of fifty-four in the midst of the Victorian era, sometimes was called upon to consume three to four feasts a day in his capacity as *quatorzième.* This was no small feat back in the days of ten-course meals washed down with half a dozen wines: White wine with the oysters, sherry with the soup, champagne with the fish, claret with the roast and game, port with the cheese, and Madeira with the fruit.

As a practiced diner, Malkeith knew how to "order and husband your topics like the courses that come before you. . . . Let them be light at first and more substantial as you proceed. . . ." During the soup course he would remain almost silent, preoccupied with the task at hand. By the next course, his appetite somewhat abated, he would proffer a short, lively anecdote. "But don't bother the mind with any serious work to do . . ." advises one author. Only as the courses advance could he become philosophic, "for all are becoming emancipated from the dominion of physical appetite, and the mental is now decidedly in the ascendant."

When the ripened fruit was set upon the table, and the servants had departed, now came time to "let flow your raciest thoughts. . . ." Malkeith would catch the subtle glance between the hostess and the female guest of honor, and he would rise with the other gentlemen for "this often tedious interval" when the ladies were banished to the drawing room and the men indulged in cigars and liqueurs, although refined "gentlemen left in the dining-room seldom or never carry the joys of wine drinking too far," stresses one book, "and no danger of conflagration or breakage arises from an over-exhilarated diner's sudden disappearance under the board, carrying with him cloth and lights and precious crystal bottles in his exit from view."

"A dinner invitation, once accepted, is a sacred obligation. If you die before the dinner takes place, your executor must attend the dinner."

SOCIETY AS I HAVE FOUND IT
Ward McAllister, 1890

"A vacant chair at a dinner party is a melancholy spectacle."

CORRECT SOCIAL USAGE, vol. II
Margaret Watts Livingston, et al., 1906

"Background music in the dining room is suitable only for resort hotels and ocean liners."

ENTERTAINING WITH ELEGANCE
Geneviève Antoine Dariaux, 1965

"Never chase a few peas or break crumbs around your plate as an idle accompaniment to your conversation."

IF YOU PLEASE!
Betty Allen and Mitchell Pirie Briggs, 1942

"Certain daring necklines have a paralyzing effect on the conversation and even on the appetite of the other dinner party guests, who hope to see a little more than is already revealed and would love to change places with the waiter, who has a particularly stimulating view."

ACCENT ON ELEGANCE
Geneviève Antoine Dariaux, 1970

"Never utter a syllable, nor look a glance of reproof at a guest. Let him break, let him shatter a vase, if he will; the repose of the hostess must cling round you still. Let a guest be late, or early, or disobliging, or rude; you must not show so much as one iota of displeasure with him. See claret staining your best embroidered tablecloth, and smile; regard the wreck of a Salviati goblet and four sherry glasses without wincing. Sheath your face in a casing of imper-

"Certain daring necklines have a paralyzing effect on the conversation and even on the appetite of the other dinner party guests, who hope to see a little more than is already revealed and would love to change places with the waiter, who has a particularly stimulating view."

turbable good nature when Norah or the man 'had in' spills peas down your bare neck and ruins your gown with trailing soup. Be concerned only if they do it to somebody else. Then look worried to death."

ETIQUETTE FOR AMERICANS
By a Woman of Fashion, 1909

"Of all things horrible, the professional talker at a table is the 'limit.' Just as you are interested in a fine jovial *tête-à-tête*—just growing very pleasing—a manly voice is heard above the murmuring din, beginning an anecdote or relating a professional experience of his own, which you have seen in newspapers, and rooted out of bound volumes of *Punch* years before. He is at times pathetic; he tries to make people weep, while inwardly they rage, and want to bite him."

ETIQUETTE FOR AMERICANS
By a Woman of Fashion, 1898

"If someone at a dinner party ever begins to tell a story and everybody stops listening after the first five minutes, and if you want to do your good deed for the day, continue to listen to the speaker attentively, nodding your head in approval from time to time; it is extremely rude to leave somebody in the lurch, talking to himself."

ACCENT ON ELEGANCE
Geneviève Antoine Dariaux, 1970

"Nothing is less alluring than a smile flavored with parsley or veal Marengo."

ACCENT ON ELEGANCE
Geneviève Antoine Dariaux, 1970

DINNER'S END

The finger bowl was a source of uneasiness to many a newly made millionaire. "[H]owever strong and virile their natures," observes an author, these entrepreneurs "become utterly helpless and panic-stricken at the mere sight of a gold finger bowl. . . ." It was easy to be confused by this mysterious bowl of water, with its decorative slice of lemon, placed before one near the meal's end. One could understand the gentleman who, having mistaken it for a bowl of lemonade, looked up in consternation after a sip: "Well! if this isn't the poorest lemonade I ever tasted!" When it comes to the finger bowl, just remember: One hand at a time and fingertips only. And as with all dining dilemmas, when in doubt glance surreptitiously sideways, then follow one's neighbor.

"Always swallow your food before leaving the table."

GOOD MANNERS FOR ALL OCCASIONS
Margaret E. Sangster, 1921

"When dinner is over, and you see that nearly all the company, except two or three, have left the table, it is not well to be one of that two or three, and to remain to an indefinite period, loitering over the last pickings of a plate of nuts. . . . Even the attraction of a beau drinking his wine beside her, ought not to induce a young lady to outstay all the company, with the pretext of being passionately fond of nuts. She may indulge this passion at any time by keeping a bag of them in her own room."

MISS LESLIE'S BEHAVIOUR BOOK
Miss Leslie, 1859

"None but a low-bred clown will ever carry fruit or *bon bons* away from the table."

FROST'S LAWS AND BY-LAWS OF AMERICAN SOCIETY
S. A. Frost, 1869

"In purchasing almond bonbons for the dinner table the hostess should make sure to select the mauve species. No one ever eats them. A dishful of the white variety will sometimes vanish in a night, but the mauve go on forever."

MANNERS FOR THE METROPOLIS
Francis W. Crowninshield, 1909

Chapter 4

MANNERS
FOR WALTZERS
AND WALLFLOWERS
And Other Visitors

ARRIVING IN STYLE

If a visitor was informed that "Madame is not at home," it was not enough to simply leave one's calling card on the silver tray and depart.

"Nothing better shows the standing of ladies or gentlemen, or their familiarity with the usages of the best society, than their use of cards," declares a writer. "The quality of the card, its size and style, the hour and manner in which it is left—all these convey a silent message to the experienced eye which indicates the character of the caller."

"Good taste never touches extremes . . ." explains a colleague, and the calling card left by the proper person was "unexceptionable" in every way. It was "neither too small, so that its recipients shall say to themselves, 'A whimsical person,' nor too large to suggest ostentation." Its typeface was plain and simple, and never approximated the owner's signature: "Autograph visiting cards are conceited affectations," denounces an authority, particularly if the facsimile engraved in gilt belonged to a man of little standing. Still worse was a photograph calling card. That was "a vulgarism," pronounces a writer, and a danger as well he warns: "If you are a gentleman, your visage may be reserved by the chambermaid, to exhibit as 'one of her beaux' . . ."

Calling cards had an elaborate and secret language that had to be mastered. If a lady caller folded over the upper left-hand corner of her card, it meant it was a visit of "felicitation." If she folded over the lower left-hand corner, it meant it was a call of "condolence." And if she folded over the entire right-hand side, it meant the card was brought in person and was not delivered by her servant.

"[W]ith the perverse ingenuity in which the human mind delights," complains an author, "mankind, or rather womankind, has involved even this apparently innocent ceremony in a large amount of red tape and confusion." Even the number of cards that were left behind was telling. If the visitor was a married woman, calling upon a widow or a spinster, she was to leave one of her cards and one of her husband's. But if she was calling upon a married matron, she was to leave one of her cards and *two* of her husband's. If the married matron was entertaining a female visitor, the caller was to leave two of her cards and *three* of her husband's, but if the visitor was masculine, she was to leave only one of her cards and three of her husband's.

It was not permissible for a confused caller to throw up her hands and say she couldn't be bothered, there were more important things to think about. Visitors, take heed: "A good memory for these trifles is one of the marks of good breeding."

"When bent on paying calls, first don one of your prettiest gowns, then arm yourself with a liberal supply of small-talk and sally forth unafraid."

ETIQUETTE FOR WOMEN
G. R. M. Devereux, 1902

"Visitors should furnish themselves with cards. Gentlemen ought simply to put their cards into their pocket, but ladies may carry them in a small elegant portfolio, called a card-case. This they can hold in their hand and it will contribute essentially (with an elegant handkerchief of embroidered cambric,) to give them an air of good taste."

DECORUM
Anonymous, 1877

"A gentleman should simply carry his cards in his pocket. The use of a card-case would give him the air of a fop."

THE MANNERS THAT WIN
Anonymous, 1880

"Even so simple a thing as extracting a card from a card-case a novice sometimes finds difficult of accomplishment; the thin card eludes gloved fingers, or two or three stick together. It is always wise to place one or two cards, or the exact number which may be required, in a separate and easily get-at-able position, for the eye of the servant is often critical and merciless, and you may feel sure that she has no opinion of the bungling, flustered card-leaver."

ETIQUETTE FOR WOMEN
G. R. M. Devereux, 1902

"[W]hen you hear the doorbell ring and glimpse an unwelcome silhouette on your doorstep, it is undeniably more elegant to go to the door and make your excuses in person, rather than to hide behind the curtains and pretend that nobody is at home."

ENTERTAINING WITH ELEGANCE
Geneviève Antoine Dariaux, 1965

"Never peer at a caller suspiciously through a crack."

THE NEW ETIQUETTE
Margery Wilson, 1940

"On opening the front door open it wide, unless you fear burglars and such-like people. To open it a few inches and then to put your head out shows that you have not much idea of the look of things."

THINGS THAT ARE NOT DONE
Edgar and Diana Woods, 1937

•   •   •

"It would be extremely clownish to carry dirt on one's shoes into a decent house, especially on a ceremonious visit; and, when there is much mud, or when we cannot walk with skill, it is proper to go in a carriage or at least to put in requisition the services of a shoeblack at a short distance from the house."

THE GENTLEMAN AND LADY'S BOOK OF POLITENESS
Mme. Celnart, 1835

"Enter a room as if you felt yourself entitled to a welcome, but wished to take no undue advantage of it."

SOCIAL ETIQUETTE
Maud C. Cooke, 18—

"Don't sidle into a room as if you had just robbed the silver chest."

ETIQUETTE FOR MODERNS
Gloria Goddard, 1941

"Don't, on the other hand, make an entrance. The woman who pauses in the doorway, a hand laid with affected grace on the door frame, and waits until all eyes are turned to her, then glides into the room is certainly attracting attention, but it is not the sort of attention she thinks it is. If she could hear the remarks made behind her back, she would change her tactics and enter a room like a human being and not like the villainess of an eighteenth-century melodrama."

ETIQUETTE FOR MODERNS
Gloria Goddard, 1941

"A lady should conquer a habit of breathing hard, or coming in very hot, or even looking very blue and shivery."

THE HABITS OF GOOD SOCIETY
Anonymous, 1859

"Don't sidle into a room as if you
had just robbed the silver chest."

"No well-bred man or woman attempts to back out of a drawing-room."

ENCYCLOPAEDIA OF ETIQUETTE
Emily Holt, 1901

LEASHED ACCESSORIES

"At a house party," reports a writer, "every lady of prominence is sure to bring at least one Pomeranian dog. Many think it wiser to bring a black and a brown, so that, no matter what gown they may wear, one of the darlings is sure not to clash with it." Although the twosome may make a striking pose while descending the staircase, the dog's mistress has committed an unpardonable faux pas, declares another: "The guest must not think that an invitation to her includes her dog."

This rule applied to short calls as well as to house stays. A dog lover was not to arrive swathed in mink, her pooch dressed identically. "[P]lease, if you really love your dog," pleads one author, "don't buy him a mink. You would only make him—and yourself—ridiculous; and besides, he would so much rather have a present of a rubber ball."

Even mink could not mask a malcontent, particularly if it was a poodle. "Poodles are generally peevish, whining, and snappish, prone to get under chairs and bite at feet, and to writhe about the skirts of dresses," declares one author, who continues, ruthlessly: "Their faces often look old, withered, cross, and blear-eyed, seeming as if constantly troubled by the hair that dangles uncomfortably in their eyes; and they are seldom healthy."

But even the most ingratiating canine could have dusty feet or a penchant for velvet sofas, so it was best to heed the rules of *Polite Society:* "Dogs have no place in a parlor," and leave one's pet at home. "Besides," adds a practical author, "your friend may have a favorite cat already established before the fire, and in that case a battle may ensue."

"Perhaps the greatest damage that most of us are ever asked to bear is that caused by a lap dog which is taken everywhere and allowed to run free because of its owner's bland unawareness that, although it may be house-trained in its own home, all strange places are 'outdoor places' to it, and the chairs and sofas in a strange house are all 'trees in the street.' "

ETIQUETTE
Emily Post, 1950

"The family dog is a very hard case to manage. If he be ugly, and frighten you, go around him cautiously; if he be dirty and offensive, and if, like Macbeth's crime, 'he smell to heaven,' never speak of it. A family are always sensitive on this point. They will defend the dog at the cost of their lives, and as a guest, if you would preserve your popularity, do you also defend, praise and endure the family dog."

ETIQUETTE, THE AMERICAN CODE OF MANNERS
Mrs. M. E. W. Sherwood, 1884

"If a guest has any actual physical aversion to pets, it is best for him to tell the hostess in advance. I knew a woman who fainted at the sight of a bird. You may say it was silly, but nevertheless, the fact remained."

MRS. OLIVER HARRIMAN'S BOOK OF ETIQUETTE
Mrs. Oliver Harriman, 1942

NERVOUS HABITS

The pipe, notes a male etiquette book author, "is the worst rival a woman can have: and it is one whose eyes she cannot scratch out; who improves with age, while she herself declines; who has an art which no woman possesses, that of never wearying her devotee; who is silent, yet a companion; costs little, yet gives much pleasure; who, lastly, never upbraids, and always yields the same joy." He concludes, in sympathy: "No wonder they hate it, dear creatures. . . ."

The diplomatic gentleman learned to conceal his devotion to weed before entering the society of women. Etiquette books offered tips for this deception, varying from chewing common parsley to gargling with water and cologne. Young ladies, in turn, were warned of the dangers of dallying with a tobaccophile, one book even offering a sample letter to follow when refusing the stained and yellowed hand of a smoker in marriage.

For the dangers of tobacco were not just upon the body but upon the soul. The boy who used tobacco in any form, reveals an etiquette expert, "loses his manliness and vigor, his sense of right and wrong becomes perverted, and his ambition leaves him." "Few are aware of the influence upon morals exerted by that filthy habit, tobacco-using," agrees another writer. "The lecherous day-dreams in which many smokers indulge, are a species of fornication for which even a brute ought to blush, if such a crime were possible for a brute. The mental libertine does not confine himself to bagnios and women of the town. In the foulness of his imagination, he invades the sanctity of virtue wherever his erotic fancy leads him." Young ladies, stay away from even the most unseasoned user, for the habit "[w]hen acquired early . . . excites the undeveloped organs, arouses the passions, and in a few years converts the once chaste and pure youth into a veritable volcano of lust, belching out from its inner fires of passion torrents of obscenity and the sulphurous fumes of lasciviousness."

"Women who smoke must drink something stronger than tea."

ADVICE TO YOUNG LADIES *from* The London Journal *of 1855 and 1862*
Selected by R. D., 1933

"[B]reak the wartime habit of furtively slipping one lone cigarette from a package hidden deep out of sight. Whenever you want a cigarette, take the package *out*."

ESQUIRE ETIQUETTE
The Editors of Esquire *magazine, 1953*

•   •   •

"When acquired early, [smoking] excites the undeveloped organs, arouses the passions, and in a few years converts the once chaste and pure youth into a veritable volcano of lust, belching out from its inner fires of passion torrents of obscenity and the sulphurous fumes of lasciviousness."

"[N]othing is so sickening to leave behind as a souvenir of yourself as the stump of an extremely dead cigar."

THE CORRECT THING
William Oliver Stevens, 1934

"It is a sign of low-breeding to fidget with the hat, cane or parasol during a call. They are introduced merely as signs that the caller is in walking dress, and are not intended, the hat to be whirled round the top of the cane, the cane to be employed in tracing out the pattern of the carpet, or the parasol to be tapped on the teeth, or worse still, sucked."

FROST'S LAWS AND BY-LAWS OF AMERICAN SOCIETY
S. A. Frost, 1869

"Avoid restlessness in company, lest you make the whole party as fidgety as yourself."

MARTINE'S HAND-BOOK OF ETIQUETTE
Arthur Martine, 1866

"Don't fold your arms across your chest and hug yourself—this makes you look tense and aloof."

THIS WAY, PLEASE
Eleanor Boykin, 1940

"When in Company, put not your Hands to any Part of the Body, not usualy Discovered."

GEORGE WASHINGTON'S RULES OF CIVILITY AND DECENT BEHAVIOUR IN
COMPANY AND CONVERSATION
Edited by Charles Moore, 1747; 1926

•   •   •

"Boring the ears with the fingers, chafing the limbs, sneezing with unnecessary sonorousness, and even a too fond and ceaseless caressing of the moustache, are in bad taste."

THE AMERICAN GENTLEMAN'S GUIDE TO POLITENESS AND FASHION
Henry Lunettes, 1863

"[W]hen you have blown your nose, you should not open your handkerchief and inspect it, as though pearls or rubies had dropped out of your skull. Such behaviour is nauseating and is more likely to lose us the affection of those who love us than to win us the favour of others."

GALATEO *OR* THE BOOK OF MANNERS
Giovanni Della Casa, 1558; translated by R. S. Pine-Coffin, 1958

"It is a breach of etiquette to assume a lazy, lounging attitude in company. If any one is too weak or too ill to sit up and assume a proper position, he had better stay at home until he is stronger or in better health."

FROST'S LAWS AND BY-LAWS OF AMERICAN SOCIETY
S. A. Frost, 1869

"[Y]ou will be careful not to sit down in a chair which you know to be the one in which the lady or gentleman of the house usually sits, even though they are absent. Many persons would just as soon see a stranger using their toothbrush, as sitting in the chair which they always occupy themselves."

THE PERFECT GENTLEMAN
By a Gentleman, 1860

THE ART OF MINGLING

When a gentleman was introduced to a lady she could repeat his name, but she should not murmur that she was "happy" or "delighted" to make his acquaintance. "The pleasure is supposed to be upon his part, the condescension upon her side," instructs an author.

It was the lady's prerogative to bow or to shake hands. Unmarried ladies were urged not to engage in the latter activity "indiscriminately." "Ladies never shake hands with gentlemen unless under circumstances of great intimacy," reminds an author.

Once a lady offered her hand, she was to give it with enthusiasm, for nothing was worse than when "a limp, nerveless something is dropped into our outstretched palm, which shows no sign of life while in our possession." Hand-shaking is a two-person operation: "[B]y all means, do not offer your hand limply and allow the other person to shake it without any participation on your part," comments a writer.

Arm movement was essential to a pleasant handshake, but that didn't justify all manner of motion. Particularly exasperating was "the melancholy style, where the hand is heaved up once or twice slowly and lowered despairingly." But equally distressing was rapid movement, where the hand was "shaken violently sideways, as though it were being used to clean a spot out of the atmosphere." It wasn't even nice to give a single toss, as if ringing the dinner bell.

Most important was to know when to quit. "[T]he worst hand is the one that stays. You have no idea what to do with it," bemoans an author. "Your own grasp is loosening and the other seems in danger of falling to the earth, and at last, as you are getting red with embarrassment and annoyance it drops nervelessly from your clasp."

"As for the cold-blooded creatures who austerely offer one or two fingers I recommend you to ignore them; look loftily over them as if unconscious of their existence and—their fingers."

THE STANDARD BOOK ON POLITENESS, GOOD BEHAVIOR AND
SOCIAL ETIQUETTE
Anonymous, 1884

"But when a lady (and more particularly a fair one) does you the honor to offer her hand, take it with an air of grateful deference which will show how

"Ladies never shake hands with gentlemen unless under circumstances of great intimacy."

you appreciate the honor; do not drop it instantly as if the touch scared you, nor hold it so long as to cause her a feeling of uneasiness."

THE STANDARD BOOK ON POLITENESS, GOOD BEHAVIOR AND
SOCIAL ETIQUETTE
Anonymous, 1884

"No thoroughbred lady would ever refuse to shake any hand that is honorable, not even the hand of a coal heaver at the risk of her fresh white glove."

ETIQUETTE
Emily Post, 1922

"A sudden and complete silence should never follow an introduction."

GEMS OF DEPORTMENT
Anonymous, 1880

"[T]o shrink away to a side-table, and affect to be absorbed in some album or illustrated work, or to cling to some unlucky acquaintance, as a drowning man clings to a spar, are *gaucheries* no shyness can excuse. Neither should a man stand too long in the same spot. To be afraid to move from one drawing-room to another is the sure sign of a neophyte in society."

GOOD MANNERS
Anonymous, 1870

"Do not say to your host or hostess that you do not like any of their friends."

OUR DEPORTMENT
Compiled by John H. Young, 1881

"Never affect a foolish reserve in mixed company, keeping aloof from others as if in a state of mental abstraction. If your brain is so full and so busy that you cannot attend to the little civilities, cheerful chit-chat, and light amusements of society, keep out of it."

THE LADIES' BOOK OF ETIQUETTE, AND MANUAL OF POLITENESS
Florence Hartley, 1873

"The members of an invited family should never be seen conversing one with another at a party."

HOW TO BEHAVE
Anonymous, 1856

"If at any morning or evening party you meet a distinguished guest, it is ill-bred to follow him from one place to another, listening to every word he utters, and making him have the uncomfortable sensation of being 'stared at.' "

FROST'S LAWS AND BY-LAWS OF AMERICAN SOCIETY
S. A. Frost, 1869

"It is unwise to invite your psychiatrist to your parties and other social events."

ETIQUETTE ETC.
Sheila Ostrander, 1967

AMATEUR SOPRANOS

"Many accomplishments are necessary for the complete success of a young lady in society," declares an authority on etiquette. The cultured lass should know how to enter a room, how to perform a graceful salutation, and how to be an artist at her toilet. She should know a little French and German and be educated enough to be "mentally appreciative." She should be able to discuss the merits of different styles of music modestly and intelligently, and she should be able to play some instrument, although she need not be a "star" performer. "Many young girls sing simple ballads and folk-songs under the moon to the tinkling of the guitar, and every one is pleased," observes an author.

Well, not everyone. "I don't think there is a great deal gained by a woman's being able to make an alarming jangle on the piano-forte, particularly under that unmerciful scheme of 'Duets,' in which two tyrants are enabled to belabour the machine at the same time," complains Lord Chesterfield. Nor must the two ladies confuse boisterous applause with the urge to continue. "[A] performance, the beginning of which was hailed with delight, may be applauded at its conclusion chiefly because it has been concluded," reveals an author.

To force every woman, talented or not, to cultivate an art is foolish, one writer protests, and merely "resulted in the torture of many innocent persons who were compelled to look at crude sketches, to admire grotesque embroideries and to listen to mediocre performances on the piano." While these skills may have helped a fair miss secure a spouse, once he carried her across the threshold his values changed: "A husband soon becomes tired of grand performances on the piano, of crotchet and worsted work, and of other fiddle-faddle employments . . ." observes an author. "A man is, in general, better pleased when he has a good dinner upon his table than when his wife speaks Greek," agrees Dr. Samuel Johnson.

"Do not by extravagant applause encourage parlor recitations, for mediocre talent is always profuse."

THE ETIQUETTE OF TO-DAY
Edith B. Ordway, 1920

"It is very impolite to speak disparagingly of the piano, however much it may be out of tune, or however inferior it may be. More especially is it a breach of etiquette to draw unfavorable comparisons between the instrument and another elsewhere."

HILL'S MANUAL OF SOCIAL AND BUSINESS FORMS
Thos. E. Hill, 1882

"A gentleman must avoid those songs which the music and the words point out as specifically composed for the softer sex. Imagine, for instance, the sweet sounds of 'Love not,' 'I dreamed that I dwelt in marble halls,' or 'Alice Gray,' issuing from a mouth surrounded with black whiskers, and buried in moustaches."

THE STANDARD BOOK ON POLITENESS, GOOD BEHAVIOR AND
SOCIAL ETIQUETTE
Anonymous, 1884

"If a guest has any actual physical aversion to pets, it is best for him to tell the hostess in advance. I knew a woman who fainted at the sight of a bird. You may say it was silly, but nevertheless, the fact remained."

"A man singing before ladies must remember their nerves, and modulate his voice."

THE HABITS OF GOOD SOCIETY
Anonymous, 1859

"There are many young women, who, when they sit down to the piano to sing, twist themselves into so many contortions, and writhe their bodies and faces about into such actions and grimaces, as would almost incline one to believe that they are suffering great bodily torture. Their bosoms heave, their shoulders shrug, their heads swing to the right and left, their lips quiver, their eyes roll; they sigh, they pant, they seem ready to expire! And what is this all about? They are merely playing a favorite concerto, or singing a new Italian song."

MANNERS, CULTURE AND DRESS OF THE BEST AMERICAN SOCIETY
Richard A. Wells, 1890

"Some people look quite savage when singing; and when rendering passages of love and tenderness, their features are far more indicative of rage, revenge and murder! . . . [T]o this end practice before a looking-glass will be found very helpful."

COLLIER'S CYCLOPEDIA OF COMMERCIAL AND SOCIAL INFORMATION
Compiled by Nugent Robinson, 1882

"Life is too short and its duties too momentous for a girl to spend years in acquiring proficiency in the production of a mere sound, and one in which, in spite of her culture, she is discounted by the ordinary canary bird."

OUR HOME
C. E. Sargent, 1883

BALLROOM BEHAVIOR

The ballroom wall was a young woman's fate, unless rescued by a trousered companion. Her chances for deliverance were determined largely by the social graces of the men in attendance. "[T]he well-bred and amiable man will sacrifice himself to those plain, ill-dressed, dull-looking beings who cling to the wall, unsought and despairing," instructs a writer. Severely criticized were those masculine guests with the "odious and selfish habit of not dancing if they cannot secure just the partners they want, and of standing, a black-coated and dismal group, like so many crows, around the doorway," replying to the hostess wandering past, "No, thanks, I don't dance," or concealing this deficiency by hiding out in the smoking room. Still worse was the dancing enthusiast so proficient that he felt he wasn't in need of a partner. "It is not the correct thing for a gentleman to dance 'stag,' that is to say, dance alone, during a cotillion where some of the ladies have no partners," scolds a writer.

Out on the dance floor gentlemen were "earnestly advised not to limit their conversation to remarks on the weather and the heat of the room" one book urges, but this was often difficult, particularly when whirling past the shrubbery behind which was concealed a small orchestra abandoning decorum in their efforts to be heard. "Loud strains and *crescendos* that force guests to elevate their voices and turn conversation into a furious babel, are to be avoided," instructs a writer.

The moment the music paused, the gentleman was to immediately remove his arm, for a woman's waist was "sacred," defends a writer, and requires "the utmost delicacy in touching." Now was the time to hand the girl back to her chaperon, unless the refreshment room was suggested as an excuse to linger together longer. This would be located on the same floor as the ballroom in a wise hostess's house, "in order that the ladies may be spared all risk from draughty staircases."

After stuffing the young lady with game pies, terrapin, trifle, tipsy cake, and bonbons, the attentive gentleman was not to be surprised when his partner failed to greet him during walking hours in the park the next day. "An introduction given for the mere purpose of enabling a lady and gentleman to go through a dance together does not constitute an acquaintanceship," explains one author. "The lady is at liberty to pass the gentleman in the park the next day without recognition."

"[I]t is a refined act of courtesy to stop the clocks when you give a big party."

ACCENT ON ELEGANCE
Geneviève Antoine Dariaux, 1970

"A gentleman intending to dance should remove his sword, otherwise he should not do so."

MANNERS AND RULES OF GOOD SOCIETY
A Member of the Aristocracy, 1901

"Should there be dancing, gentlemen may don their gloves, the reason being obvious. . . . For a man to dance with a lady and leave the imprints of his fingers upon her dress is anything but creditable to him. . . . Above all things, men should bear in mind that women rule and sway society, and the man who incurs, in any manner, their dislike or enmity, is one of the most unfortunate of individuals who will find that the road he expected would be lined on either side with beautiful, blooming roses is in reality bordered by shrubbery of which the most conspicuous characteristics are sharp, protuberant and long-stemmed thorns."

THE NEW CENTURY PERFECT SPEAKER
Edited by John Coulter, 1901

"Cavalry officers should never wear spurs in a ball-room."

MIXING IN SOCIETY
*The Right Hon. The Countess of *******, 1869*

"Ladies should not cross the ball-room alone. It invites attention."

SOCIAL ETIQUETTE
Maud C. Cooke, 18—

"Dance with grace and modesty . . . refrain
from great leaps and ridiculous jumps. . . ."

"Beware of presenting to ladies, in balls or assemblies a box of *bonbons,* under penalty of having the air of a caricature."

THE GENTLEMAN AND LADY'S BOOK OF POLITENESS
Mme. Celnart, 1835

"It is not the correct thing for a lady to refuse the invitation of one gentleman, and then accept that of another for the same dance. Duels have been fought for smaller matters than this."

THE CORRECT THING IN GOOD SOCIETY
Florence Howe Hall, 1902

"On the Continent, however intimate, he must never dance twice with the same lady, that is, if she be unmarried. Mamma would interfere, and ask his intentions if he did so."

THE HABITS OF GOOD SOCIETY
Anonymous, 1859

"During the dance all should be exclusively devoted to their partners, and never allow themselves to keep up, by conversation or the telegraph of the eye and face, a communication with others."

THE BAZAR BOOK OF DECORUM
Anonymous, 1870

"Never make arrangements for the next dance while another is in progress."

THE MANNERS THAT WIN
Anonymous, 1880

"Don't dance with your wife just once and then park her for the rest of the evening."

SOCIAL DANCING
Prepared by Arthur Murray, 1932

"If a lady waltz with you, beware not to press her waist; you must only lightly touch it with the palm of your hand, lest you leave a disagreeable impression not only on her *ceinture,* but on her mind."

MARTINE'S HAND-BOOK OF ETIQUETTE
Arthur Martine, 1866

"Avoid confidential conversation in a ball room. It is out of season, and in excessively bad taste."

THE LADIES' BOOK OF ETIQUETTE, AND MANUAL OF POLITENESS
Florence Hartley, 1873

"Dance with grace and modesty, neither affect to make a parade of your knowledge; refrain from great leaps and ridiculous jumps, which would attract the attention of all towards you."

DECORUM
Anonymous, 1877

"Do not pride yourself on doing the "steps neatly," unless you are ambitious of being taken for a dancing-master; between whose motions and those of a *gentleman* there is a great difference."

THE PERFECT GENTLEMAN
By a Gentleman, 1860

"The tendency to slide the feet across a slippery floor should be curbed."

THE BOOK OF GOOD MANNERS
Victor H. Diescher, 1923

"It is not the correct thing for two gentlemen who have collided in the waltz, or who have caused their partners to do so, to glare silently and wrathfully at each other."

THE CORRECT THING IN GOOD SOCIETY
Florence Howe Hall, 1902

"Do not be the last to leave the ball room. It is more elegant to leave early, as staying too late gives others the impression that you do not often have an invitation to a ball, and must 'make the most of it.' "

THE GENTLEMEN'S BOOK OF ETIQUETTE AND MANUAL OF POLITENESS
Cecil B. Hartley, 1860

"It would be hard on the lady of the house if everybody leaving a large ball thought it necessary to wish her good-night. In quitting a small dance, however, a parting bow is expected. It is then that the pretty daughter of the house gives you that sweet smile of which you dream afterwards in a gooseberry nightmare of 'tum-tum-tiddy-tum,' and waltzes *à deux temps,* and masses of tarlatane and bright eyes, flushed cheeks and dewy glances. See them to-morrow, my dear fellow, it will cure you."

THE HABITS OF GOOD SOCIETY
Anonymous, 1859

"As to masked balls, it is an amusement altogether to be condemned."

THE GENTLEMAN AND LADY'S BOOK OF POLITENESS
Mme. Celnart, 1835

Chapter 5

MANNERS
FOR PREENERS
AND DANDIES

And Other Well-Appareled

A MAN OF STYLE

"A man's wardrobe is now almost as varied as a woman's," reports a writer in 1897. "He has different costumes for walking, riding, driving, visiting, boating, hunting, shooting, golfing, bicycling, tennis, and cricket, dining, smoking, and lounging, football, racing, and yachting, to say nothing of uniform and Court suit, besides the now developing motor-car costume."

With such a wide variety of outfits to choose from, it was tempting for a man to indulge in a bit of vanity. But don't be continually brushing imaginary crumbs off your trousers or checking your reflection in every passing window, warn the writers. Take note: It "is the apparent consciousness of being dressed that often betrays the novelty of a person's condition."

The truly affluent shunned outward displays of prosperity, for they didn't need to advertise their standing in life. "It is bad taste to dress in the extreme of fashion; and, in general, those only do so who have no other claim to distinction—leave it, in these times, to shopmen and pickpockets," advises one writer.

In any case there was a certain charm to an old familiar jacket. "The best coats in our streets are worn on the backs of penniless fops, broken down merchants, clerks with pitiful salaries, and men that do not pay up," contends one book. Quite so, agrees another: "There is more honour in an old hunting-coat than in a new one, in a uniform with a bullet-hole in it than one without. . . ."

But there was a degree of casualness that a gentleman should not dip below. He must never descend to "the slouchy appearance of a half-unbuttoned vest, and suspenderless pantaloons. That sort of affectation is, if possible, even more disgusting than the painfully elaborate frippery of the dandy or dude." Whether dressed formally or informally, the rule was simply this: "A gentleman should always be so well dressed that his dress shall never be observed at all."

"A man who is badly dressed, feels chilly, sweaty, and prickly. He stammers, and does not always tell the truth. He means to, perhaps, but he can't."

SEARCH LIGHTS ON HEALTH
Prof. B. G. Jefferis and J. L. Nichols, 1896

"A gentleman faultlessly gloved cannot go far wrong."

SOCIAL ETIQUETTE
Maud C. Cooke, 18—

"It was at one time the fashion to affect a certain negligence, which was called poetic, and supposed to be the result of genius. An ill-tied, if not positively untied cravat was a sure sign of an unbridled imagination; and a waistcoat was held together by one button only, as if the swelling soul in the wearer's bosom had burst all the rest. If in addition to this the hair was unbrushed and curly, you were certain of passing for a 'man of soul.' I should not recommend any young gentleman to adopt this style, unless indeed he can mouth a great deal, and has a good stock of quotations from the poets. It is of no use to show me the clouds, unless I can positively see you in them, and no amount of negligence in your dress and person will convince me you are a genius, unless you produce an octavo volume of poems published by yourself."

THE HABITS OF GOOD SOCIETY
Anonymous, 1859

"A rich man may be forgiven for wearing a threadbare coat, but a poor man is inexcusable for appearing in fine broadcloth and dressing his wife and daughters in silks, velvets and diamonds."

THE LADIES' AND GENTLEMEN'S ETIQUETTE
Mrs. E. B. Duffey, 1877

"[D]on't dress like a 'dude,' or a 'swell,' nor carry a little poodle dog (a man's glory is in his strength and manliness—not in aping silly girls), nor cock your hat on one side, nor tip it back on your head (let it sit straight and square), nor wear anything conspicuous or that will make you offensive to others."

MODERN MANNERS AND SOCIAL FORMS
Julia M. Bradley, 1889

"A snuff box, watch, studs, sleeve-buttons, watch-chain, and one ring are all the jewelry a well-dressed man can wear."

THE GENTLEMEN'S BOOK OF ETIQUETTE AND MANUAL OF POLITENESS
Cecil B. Hartley, 1860

"Very big canes are in very bad taste, especially for young men."

HOW TO BEHAVE AND HOW TO AMUSE
G. H. Sandison, 1895

THE HATLESS MAN

"Most of us can remember the time," recalls a female etiquette writer, "when a man separated from his hat was uneasy if not actually unhappy. True, he left it in the cloakroom at a restaurant or private dance as convention prescribed, but obviously he did not want to do it." "Today men seem to be making an effort to free themselves from the tyranny of the hat," reports the author in 1940. "These, however, are the extremists or perhaps the forerunners of a new order."

Alas, they were the latter, another woman laments: "It is rather inconvenient, because the kind of hat a man wore used to give a woman a clue to help her decide, for example, whether or not she could run the risk of sharing a taxi with him during a rainstorm: if he was wearing a cap or a soft felt tilted over the eye at an exaggerated angle, it would have been preferable to get drenched; whereas a derby or a Homburg was a reassuring symbol of respectability."

Whether a man doffed his hat or not was yet another way to spot the gentleman in a crowd. Men paid dearly for this neglect: "Women seldom have bald heads, but men often do, the baldness commencing upon the head at a point which is covered by the hat," explains an author. "Baldness is usually avoided by keeping the head cool," he continues. Bare scalps, gleefully theorizes another, "may be considered, perhaps, as a sort of punishment for disregarding one of the most imperative rules of politeness, to always remove the hat in the presence of ladies. . . ." Gentlemen who regularly failed in this practice should take precautions, urged one writer, who recommended poking five hundred holes in every new hat, "so that there shall be more hole than hat."

"On the street a man should wear a hat. It completes the picture—without one a man seems to be just going across the street."

THE NEW AMERICAN ETIQUETTE
Edited by Lily Haxworth Wallace, 1941

"[D]on't dress like a 'dude,' or a 'swell,' nor . . . cock your
hat on one side, nor tip it back on your head (let it sit
straight and square), nor wear anything conspicuous or that
will make you offensive to others."

"Bravo for the men who still wear a hat! But if they fail to remove it when entering an elevator, shop, or restaurant, it would be better for a pitiless gust of wind to carry it away forever."

ELEGANCE
Geneviève Antoine Dariaux, 1964

"Only the man whose hair stays put should attempt to go hatless in town."

AMY VANDERBILT'S ETIQUETTE
Amy Vanderbilt, 1972

"If your hat blows off, never run after it. Somebody will always run after it for you."

HERBERT BEERBOHM TREE
Collected by Max Beerbohm, 1920
(From his personal notebooks)

A GENTLEMAN'S TOILET

"Let your hair be well filled with pomatum, powder, and bear's grease, and tuck it under your hat," the *London Chronicle* advised its gentlemen readers in 1787. If a dead bear was not readily available, an excellent substitute could be made by obtaining beef shank bones from the butcher, melting their marrow with yellow wax, then adding scent when cooled.

Should the mixture go rancid, don't succumb to a shampoo. "Shampooing is a great detriment to the beauty of the hair," warns an etiquette writer. "Soap fades it, often turning it yellow." If you *have* to shampoo, there are alternatives to soap and water, suggest the authors. "New England rum, constantly used to wash the hair, keeps it very clean . . ." recommends one book.

A similar hydrophobia applied to the body bath, but this was not always wise, counsels a writer: "Good health requires that the whole body be frequently and thoroughly bathed, an operation that some persons neglect entirely in winter."

While a gentleman's body may have been less than hygienic, his clothing was always spotless. It was improper to wear soiled gloves in society, and impoverished bachelors were offered this penny-saving tip for cleaning white gloves: "Put the gloves on. Have in a saucer some gasolene and wash your gloved hands in this, after which take a clean flannel rag and wipe and rub the gloves, taking care not to do this near a fire or burning gas. When quite dry, take off and pin to the curtain or where a current of air may strike them and cause the gasolene to evaporate quickly." If that doesn't work, clean the gloves with slightly damp bread crumbs, advises another. By the way, tips a writer: A banana peel is an excellent bargain polish for shoes.

"Trouser presses are no good; they are a snare and a delusion. They squeeze the life out of the exuberant and expressive trouser and leave it in a condition of impotence. Really good wool is actually alive; it must never be crushed to death. The best way to show a regard for trousers is to hang them in your wardrobe end upwards with hangers, and give them freedom to recover naturally from their exciting day."

ETIQUETTE FOR GENTLEMEN
Anonymous, 1925

"True politeness would suggest that we shall not be perfumed with cologne or musk, onions or tobacco, the odors of the hen-house or the barn."

GOOD MORALS AND GENTLE MANNERS
Alex M. Gow, 1873

"Rain-water is best for the bath."

FROST'S LAWS AND BY-LAWS OF AMERICAN SOCIETY
S. A. Frost, 1869

"Get rid at once of offensive teeth, remembering that an empty house is better than a bad tenant."

THE HEARTHSTONE; OR, LIFE AT HOME
Laura C. Holloway, 1883

"Don't neglect the small hairs that project from the nostrils and grow about the apertures of the ears—small matters of the toilet often over-looked."

DON'T

Censor, 1888

"The nose, like all other organs, augments in size by frequent handling, so we recommend every person to keep his own fingers, as well as those of his friends or enemies, away from it."

THE BAZAR BOOK OF DECORUM

Anonymous, 1870

"A man with a trivial nose should not wear a large moustache. Doing so will increase the insignificance of his insignificant nose. . . . Sometimes the ends of a man's moustache are visible to persons walking behind him. This imparts to him a belligerent, aggressive air, that makes small children refrain from asking him the time, and saves him from being asked the way by puzzled pedestrians."

ETIQUETTE FOR EVERY DAY

Mrs. Humphry, 1904

BELLE OF THE BALL

"However ugly you may be, rest assured that there is some style of habiliment which will make you passable," consoles an etiquette expert. But don't reflexively turn to the latest fashions for your salvation. "We have seen persons looking well by adopting some prevailing mode of dress, while others have looked exceedingly ill," comments an author.

Those who blindly follow fashion often do so to the detriment of their individual features. "If emerald green is the fashionable color, all of the yellowest skins will be framed in it," one writer predicts. "When hobble skirts are the thing, the fattest wabble along, looking for all the world like chandeliers tied up in mosquito netting." Far better for the rotund to forgo the excitement of the Paris runways and visit the zoo instead for inspiration. "Remember the robin has a red breast," hints an author, "while the elephant is clothed in dark

*"Only the man whose hair stays put should
attempt to go hatless in town."*

gray." Keep the ornithological flash off your head as well, suggests another: "Fat women should never wear . . . heavily feathered hats."

Dress not to impress others nor to torment them either. "Frills, and neck-laces, relieve a long neck; but short-necked ladies should avoid every thing that serves to contract the distance between the shoulders and the chin. One never sees such a figure encased in a huge frill, without feeling apprehensive of instantaneous suffocation," confesses an author.

Unfortunately, the women most in need of this advice were precisely the ones least likely to open a book, sigh the etiquette writers, for "women with brains never wear silly things."

"Never start an argument unless you are well dressed."

Unattributed quotation
IF YOU PLEASE!
Betty Allen and Mitchell Pirie Briggs, 1942

"The low-necked dress is a fatal lure to many a woman who ought to know better than to display her physical imperfections to the gaze of a pitiless world."

OUR MANNERS AND SOCIAL CUSTOMS
Daphne Dale, 1891

"If a gentleman requests the pleasure of a lady's company to the opera, she has no right to turn that expected pleasure into a pain and mortification by pre-senting herself with tumbled hair, ill-chosen dress, badly-fitting gloves and an atmosphere of cheap and offensive perfumes."

THE LADIES' AND GENTLEMEN'S ETIQUETTE
Mrs. E. B. Duffey, 1877

•   •   •

"Nor—as some young girls do—is it good form to carry small animal pets, guinea-pigs, lizards and the like, in the pocket of your cloak or wrap."

THE BOOK OF GOOD MANNERS
Frederick H. Martens, 1923

"It is the correct thing to remember that a woman who is pinched in at the waist with tight corsets, throttled around the neck with a tight collar, and cramped as to her feet with tight, high-heeled shoes, will walk about as gracefully as a swan on a turnpike-road."

THE CORRECT THING IN GOOD SOCIETY
Florence Howe Hall, 1902

"A gentleman should never attempt to step over a lady's train; he should go around it."

AS OTHERS SEE US
Anonymous, 1890

"One cannot picture a beautiful and high-bred woman, wearing a tiara and other ballroom jewels, *leaning* against anything."

ETIQUETTE
Emily Post, 1942

"To wear dresses in the home circle that have done service in the past as ball or dinner dresses, sometimes gives a tawdry, miserable look to the wearer."

SENSIBLE ETIQUETTE OF THE BEST SOCIETY
Compiled by Mrs. H. O. Ward, 1878

"A woman washing dishes in an old velvet dress looks like a slattern. She is not suitably dressed. The well-bred woman always manages to be suitably dressed, even when she is washing dishes."

ETIQUETTE FOR MODERNS
Gloria Goddard, 1941

"Sensible women do not accept the moving pictures as an index to style. The actress may be wearing gowns that are beautiful, effective, but they may not be in good taste."

THE NEW BOOK OF ETIQUETTE, vol. II
Lillian Eichler, 1924

"Though you may not know it, there are people who form their first impression of you from your heels."

EVERYDAY MANNERS
Faculty of the South Philadelphia High School for Girls, 1922

THE PERFECT ACCESSORY

"In the hands of a pretty woman a fan is eloquent . . ." praises one writer, but a fan expressed far more than beauty. Wielded aright, it signaled instructions out of earshot of the chaperon.

Touching the tip of her fan to her finger, a miss cried silently to a gentleman: "I wish to speak with you." As the obedient suitor arrived, he was warned by the fan twirled in her right hand: "We are being watched." When the coast was clear, the language of love was resumed. Drawn slowly across her cheek, the fan whispered: "I love you." And if pressed, half-opened, to the fair maiden's lips, it granted: "You may kiss me."

Such conduct was shocking, protests an etiquette writer. "Flirting a fan, or lounging, or mysterious whispers behind a fan, are all rude." Never be seen twirling your rings nor fingering your lace either. "When seated, if you are not sewing or knitting, keep your hands perfectly quiet," orders a writer. "This, whilst one of the most difficult accomplishments to attain, is the surest mark of a lady."

"A lady should wear neither bracelet nor necklace when walking in the street."

THE CORRECT THING IN GOOD SOCIETY
Florence Howe Hall, 1902

"*In the female beauty of physical development there is nothing that can equal full breasts. . . . All false forms are easily detected, because large natural ones will generally quiver and move at every step, while the artificial ones will manifest no expression of life.*"

"Only with full evening dress should a woman blaze with diamonds or drip with pearls or scintillate with rainbows of emerald, sapphire, and ruby."

VOGUE'S BOOK OF ETIQUETTE
The Editors of Vogue, *1923*

"Do not wear rings on the outside of your gloves."

INQUIRE WITHIN FOR ANYTHING YOU WANT TO KNOW
Anonymous, 1858

"No matter what the fashion may be, the gloves of a well-dressed woman are never so tight that her hands have the appearance of sausages."

THE NEW ETIQUETTE
Margery Wilson, 1940

"Economy in gloves is an insult to society."

FROST'S LAWS AND BY-LAWS OF AMERICAN SOCIETY
S. A. Frost, 1869

"Except when actually conveying food to the mouth, I don't know of any occasion when gloves cannot be worn."

THE AIR FORCE WIFE
Nancy Shea; revised by Anna Perle Smith, 1966

"A slippery envelope-purse is the liability of femininity en route."

THE NEW ETIQUETTE
Margery Wilson, 1940

"In the female beauty of physical development there is nothing that can equal full breasts. . . . All false forms are easily detected, because large natural ones will generally quiver and move at every step, while the artificial ones will manifest no expression of life."

SEARCH LIGHTS ON HEALTH
Prof. B. G. Jefferis and J. L. Nichols, 1896

"Large hats make little women look like mushrooms . . ."

EVERYDAY ETIQUETTE

Marion Harland and Virginia Van de Water, 1907

POWDER ROOM REMEDIES

"A beautiful hand is a poem in itself . . ." applauds an etiquette writer, and resourceful maidens went to great lengths to preserve this asset. "There is no end of the tricks to which they resort to render their hands delicate and beautiful," discloses one author. "Some of these devices are not only painful, but exceedingly ridiculous. For instance, I have known some of them to sleep every night with their hands held up to the bed-posts by pulleys, hoping by that means to render them pale and delicate." Others perplexed their mates by climbing into bed with oversized gloves stuffed with the remains of breakfast: "Large mittens worn at night filled with wet bran or oatmeal, keep the hands white, in spite of the disfiguring effects of house-work," tips a writer.

Still others let their days be ruled by their hands. "Many a young girl remains idle for fear her hand will grow larger by work," admits a writer in 1877. "The Early Victorian hand, small, anaemic, narrow-palmed," retorts an etiquette colleague half a century later, "is now regarded with a healthy contempt, and the hand that looks as if it can do things, whether gloveless or dressed in the glove which permits of their doing, is the hand of the hour."

Wrinkles on the face were attacked by another means. Reports a writer in 1883: "A bottle of shellac is among the toilet articles of many New York women, it is claimed, and some of them have acquired a wonderful degree of skill in using it." Their adroitness was not on the furniture but on themselves, for shellac, it was reputed, could be used to paint wrinkles out of the face. "[T]he wrinkled parts of the skin are . . . held at a sufficient tension to smooth out the wrinkles. The varnish penetrates and stiffens the skin in drying, and a smooth surface is left. . . . The drawback is that it soon cracks, roughens, and is hard to remove. A renewal is needed every day, and the result must be permanently injurious to the skin," worries the author. If that didn't work, the local butcher might have just the right face salve: "I knew many fashionable ladies in Paris who used to bind their faces, every night on going to bed, with slices of raw beef, which is said to keep the skin from wrinkles, while it gives a youthful freshness and brilliancy to the complexion. I have no doubt of its efficacy," concludes an etiquette author.

"The woman who leaves a trail of perfume in her wake is an objectionable person, and ought to be set on a desert island."

THINGS THAT ARE NOT DONE
Edgar and Diana Woods, 1937

"Excessive use of powder is also a vulgar trick. . . . Ladies sometimes catch up their powder and rub it on in a hurry, without even stopping to look in the glass, and go into company with their faces looking as though they just came out of a meal-bag. It is a ridiculous sight, and ladies may be sure it is disgusting to gentlemen."

AS OTHERS SEE US
Anonymous, 1890

"Finger-nails are another source of feminine excess. The woman who goes about her daily avocations with blood-red finger-nails is merely harking back to the days of savagery, when hands smeared with blood were a sign of successful fighting."

THINGS THAT ARE NOT DONE
Edgar and Diana Woods, 1937

"Some young ladies have a bad habit of biting their fingers, especially if they rejoice in handsome hands; and the same ladies, by way of variety, are prone to bite the corners of books, and the edges of closed fans. So it is dangerous to trust these articles in their vicinity. We have seen the corners of an elegant Annual nearly bitten off at a centre-table in the course of one evening."

MISS LESLIE'S BEHAVIOUR BOOK
Miss Leslie, 1859

"*Some young ladies . . . are prone to bite the corners of books. . . . So it is dangerous to trust these articles in their vicinity.*"

"A beautiful eyelash is an important adjunct to the eye. The lashes may be lengthened by trimming them occasionally in childhood. Care should be taken that this trimming is done neatly and evenly, and especially that the points of the scissors do not penetrate the eye."

OUR DEPORTMENT
Compiled by John H. Young, 1881

"Dark hair becomes lighter by being kept uncovered, especially in moonlight."

OF THE GOVERNMENT AND CONDUCT OF WOMEN
Francesco da Barberino, 13–; translated by W. M. Rossetti, 1869

Chapter 6

MANNERS
FOR WITS
AND RACONTEURS

And Other Conversationalists

THE TALK OF THE TOWN

"A woman cannot learn too early that her first social duty is *never to be in the way,*" commands an expert in etiquette. This restraint was especially important in conversation. It was irritating for a man to hear a woman pontificate on a masculine topic. Remember, ladies: "It is not necessary to be wise, it is only necessary to please."

The proper gentleman immediately changed the subject of conversation when joined by a lady. "All topics especially interesting to gentlemen, such as the turf, the exchange, or the farm, should be excluded from general conversation," explains a writer. The discussion of politics or religion was also taboo in front of women, as was any topic that might lead to animated disagreement. "Ladies abhor anything that looks like discussion; they are creatures of sentiment more than reason," notes a male author. "[A]greeability, rather than profundity, should be your aim, in the choice of topics," confirms another.

Yet no matter how agreeable, a topic must never begin with a query. "Never ask a lady a question about anything whatever," insists an author. Women were not the only ones exempted from this impertinence. "As a rule, *direct questions* are inadmissible in good society," explains a writer. "Some authorities in etiquette even go so far as to say that *all* questions are strictly tabooed," adds another. If a gentleman *really* wished to discover the state of a young lady's roses, he must never inquire, "How are your roses?" but must gently murmur, "I trust your roses are blooming along the walk." Stricter authorities denounced even this approach, insisting that real gentlemen would never stoop to such curious ploys but would patiently wait for the lady to volunteer. And no matter how offended she was by his query, a lady must never "show violent displeasure even when you don't like what is being said," insists a writer. "It is better to smile and change the subject."

"To invariably commence a conversation by remarks on the weather shows a poverty of ideas that is truly pitiable."

FROST'S LAWS AND BY-LAWS OF AMERICAN SOCIETY
S. A. Frost, 1869

"Death is not a proper subject for conversation with a delicate person, or shipwreck with a sea-captain's wife . . ."

THE UNIVERSAL SELF-INSTRUCTOR
Edited by Albert Ellery Berg, 1882

"We must also find fault with those people who take every opportunity to tell us of their dreams and do so with such feeling and such amazement that it is quite exhausting to listen to them, especially since they are generally the sort of people whose finest achievements would make dull listening, even if they had been awake when they performed them."

GALATEO *OR* THE BOOK OF MANNERS
Giovanni Della Casa, 1588; translated by R. S. Pine-Coffin, 1958

•   •   •

"Some persons have a mania for Greek and Latin quotations; this is particularly to be avoided. It is like pulling up the stones from a tomb wherewith to kill the living."

TREASURES OF SCIENCE, HISTORY AND LITERATURE
Moses Folsom and J. D. O'Connor, 1879

"To use a foreign phrase and then to translate it, is as much as to say your listeners are ignoramuses."

THE MANNERS THAT WIN
Anonymous, 1880

"Lawyers, literary people, military men, travellers, invalids and aged ladies, ought to have a prudent and continual distrust of the abuse of digressions."

THE GENTLEMAN AND LADY'S BOOK OF POLITENESS
Mme. Celnart, 1835

"Don't enter an argument unless you mean to follow it out till you reach the truth. To dodge and equivocate and confuse the issue may be smart, but it is not manly or honorable."

OUR MANNERS AND SOCIAL CUSTOMS
Daphne Dale, 1891

"Money is never talked of in polite society; it is taken for granted."

THE BOOK OF GOOD MANNERS
Mrs. Burton Kingsland, 1901

"When asking questions about persons who are not known to you, in a drawing-room, avoid using adjectives; or you may enquire of a mother, 'Who is that awkward, ugly girl?' and be answered, 'Sir, that is my daughter.' "

THE GENTLEMEN'S BOOK OF ETIQUETTE AND MANUAL OF POLITENESS
Cecil B. Hartley, 1860

"Prudence also advises you not to excite curiosity nor to torment people by unfinished sentences, but rather to be silent if you are not inclined to speak out. There are people who are used to give their friends such mysterious hints, as for instance: 'I have heard very unpleasant things of you, but am not at liberty to communicate to you what I have been told.' Such hints are of no use and create uneasiness."

PRACTICAL PHILOSOPHY OF SOCIAL LIFE
After the German of Baron Knigge; P. Will, 1805

"Metaphysics are as intrusive in the midst of agreeable prattle, as a skeleton at a wedding feast."

TREASURES OF SCIENCE, HISTORY AND LITERATURE
Moses Folsom and J. D. O'Connor, 1879

"The people who can be pleasantly silly, and who have a genius for talking nonsense, always get on best in society. . . . Society lives by its butterflies. They are its *raison d'être*. Rational conversation is quite out of place at a ball, a dinner, or a wedding. One has to froth one's nothings up to a pretty cream, like white of egg, and to make play with them, skip round them, dance lightly over them, and then one's reward is in hearing some one say, 'I always get on with Miss So-and-So. Not much in her, but she is pleasant and amusing.' "

ETIQUETTE FOR EVERY DAY
Mrs. Humphry, 1904

THE KING'S ENGLISH

"A man is quite sure to show his good or bad breeding the instant he opens his mouth to talk in company," claims an expert. Etiquette books taught readers how to spot those nouveaux riches: They say "mansion" instead of "big house," tips one author. They " 'arise' and 'retire'; they do not get up and go to bed," clues another. "If they have a dirty little closet, with ten valueless books in it, they will call it their *library*," scoffs a third.

"Metaphysics are as intrusive in the midst of agreeable prattle, as a skeleton at a wedding feast."

But they gave themselves away by their abbreviations. "The well-bred take all sorts of liberties with language," admits a writer, "but they know what liberties it is well bred to take. Commercial clippings of words, like ' 'phone,' 'wire,' 'photo,' 'auto,' 'ad' for advertisement, are not used by them." Nor do they repeat truncated words coined to convey leisure and luxury. "[D]o not give encouragement to that single-headed double-bodied deformity of language, 'brunch,' " instructs one book. "The syllable 'unch' is a very ugly one which furthermore has a hurried lunch-wagon suggestion unless the suffix 'eon' adds its slight fragment of grace."

Perhaps the greatest blunder was the use of slang. "Slang is indeed the weeds of speech," sniffs an author. Slang came from the most suspicious places, such as the sidewalks or, worse yet, the funny papers. Expressions that sent shivers up the alabaster spines of the well-bred were "Okey doke," "Hi ya, Toots," "Oh, yeah?" "Pipe down," "Sez you," "For crying out loud!" " '[D]umbunny,' " comments an etiquette author, is "not used by people of refinement."

Phrases used in saloons, stables, and clubs were forbidden in the presence of ladies. "If men could see the shiver of disgust which passes over a lady when they roll out an oath on the street with such gusto, they would pause ere they repeated it," reports an author. But women were also offenders: "The women who use such exclamations as 'the Dickens!' 'goodness!' 'gracious!' 'my crackey!' or others of like import, are vulgar and lacking in refinement of feeling. They often approach dangerously near to 'female swearing,' " one writer warns.

Finally, certain words were taboo because of the images they brought to mind; still, readers were cautioned: "Avoid an affectation of excessive modesty. Do not use the word 'limb' for 'leg.' If legs are really improper, then let us on no account mention them." But don't stoop to the coyness of one man, who informed a young miss that he had received a "limb-acy" from his old aunt. Such prudery was no proof of purity, ventures another: "The young lady who goes into a spasm of virtuous hysterics upon hearing the word 'leg,' is perhaps just the one who at home riots her imagination in voluptuous French novels. . . ."

"Especially is the American to be warned against an affected habit of speech. To try to talk like an Englishman is an affectation always detected. To find French more easy than American is a most transparent humbug."

ETIQUETTE, THE AMERICAN CODE OF MANNERS
Mrs. M. E. W. Sherwood, 1884

"It is a girl's part to be pretty and attractive, and coarse expressions fall from lips that have a refined and gentle look like the croak of a raven from a pretty canary."

THE MANNERS THAT WIN
Anonymous, 1880

"[D]on't affect a lisp or talk baby-talk. Somebody will probably kill you some time if you do."

COMPETE!
Frances Angell, 1935

"It is not the correct thing to blur one's words so that the sound is as of a person who speaks with his mouth full of pudding."

THE CORRECT THING IN GOOD SOCIETY
Florence Howe Hall, 1902

"If you talk sentences, do not at the same time give yourself a magisterial air in doing it."

MARTINE'S HAND-BOOK OF ETIQUETTE
Arthur Martine, 1866

"Do not, however much you may be pleased with any remark, cry out 'Bravo!' clap your hands, or permit any gesture, silent or otherwise, to mark your appreciation of it."

FROST'S LAWS AND BY-LAWS OF AMERICAN SOCIETY
S. A. Frost, 1869

"[E]xcessive gesticulators have the appearance of madmen."

THE GENTLEMAN AND LADY'S BOOK OF POLITENESS
Mme. Celnart, 1835

"Do not go into society unless you can make up your mind to be cheerful, sympathetic, animating, as well as animated. Dulness is one of the unforgivable offences. Society does not require you to be as hilarious as if you had just come into a fortune, but you have no right to look as if you had just lost one."

GOOD BEHAVIOR
Anonymous, 1876

"*Don't* be overenthusiastic. Maybe the person you are talking to is not too fond of you."

100 POINTS IN ETIQUETTE AND 101 DON'TS
K. H. and M. B. H., 1929

"Button-holding is a common but most blameable breach of good manners. If a man requires to be forcibly detained to listen to you, you are as rude in thus detaining him, as if you had put a pistol to his head and threatened to blow his brains out if he stirred."

THE GENTLEMEN'S BOOK OF ETIQUETTE AND MANUAL OF POLITENESS
Cecil B. Hartley, 1860

"I have seen many people, who, while you are speaking to them, instead of looking at, and attending to you, fix their eyes upon the ceiling, or some other part of the room, look out of the window, play with a dog, twirl their snuffbox or pick their nose. Nothing discovers a little, futile, frivolous mind, more than this, and nothing is so offensively ill-bred: it is an explicit declaration, on your part, that the most trifling object deserves your attention, more than all that can be said by the person who is speaking to you."

THE AMERICAN CHESTERFIELD
Lord Chesterfield, 18—

"[I]t is unmannerly to fall asleep, as many people do, whilst the company is engaged in conversation. . . . Besides, they are generally obliged to doze in an uncomfortable position, and this nearly always causes them to make unpleasant noises and gestures in their sleep."

"[D]on't stare impassively at the speaker as if he were a post, or assume an attitude of resignation, as if you were trying to bear the infliction patiently."

AS OTHERS SEE US
Anonymous, 1890

"[T]he direct and active sort of silent rudeness is to listen with a fixed and attentive stare on the speaker, and without any necessity of raising the eyebrows—for that might be precarious—show your utter amazement, that any one should think of thus addressing a person of your rank, wealth, genius, or greatness."

MARTINE'S HAND-BOOK OF ETIQUETTE
Arthur Martine, 1866

"[I]t is unmannerly to fall asleep, as many people do, whilst the company is engaged in conversation. Their conduct shows that they have little respect for their friends and care nothing either for them or their talk. Besides, they are generally obliged to doze in an uncomfortable position, and this nearly always causes them to make unpleasant noises and gestures in their sleep. Often enough they begin to sweat and dribble at the mouth."

GALATEO *OR* THE BOOK OF MANNERS
Giovanni Della Casa, 1558; translated by R. S. Pine-Coffin, 1958

"If there is a halting speaker, you must not move ahead of him or find his words for him, as though you had plenty to spare for his needs."

GALATEO *OR* THE BOOK OF MANNERS
Giovanni Della Casa, 1558; translated by R. S. Pine-Coffin, 1958

"Never put your cold, clammy hands on a person, saying, 'Did you ever know anyone to have such cold hands as mine?' "

MANNERS FOR MILLIONS
Sophie C. Hadida, 1932

"Don't play the Jekyll-Hyde bit on the phone: When the beautiful, delicious voice that answers the phone discovers the call is not for it, it suddenly changes to a raucous screech to summon the other person."

ETIQUETTE ETC.
Sheila Ostrander, 1967

"Never say over the telephone, 'What was the name?' The person at the other end is not yet dead . . ."

ACCENT ON ELEGANCE
Geneviève Antoine Dariaux, 1970

THE SENSITIVE ARTIST

A visit by a collector to an artist's studio was an intimidating prospect for patron and painter alike and required the tutelage of etiquette. Desperate to please, a penniless painter might spend the day before the visit memorizing the correct pronunciation for eighty well-known families offered in one book of decorum. Equally nervous, the unschooled entrepreneur, who sought to decorate the walls of his newly bought mansion, might spend the day taking a crash course in symmetry and motif. But that is gauche, charge the etiquette books: "It is unpardonable to 'cram' yourself previous to a social gathering; that is, to read up any special subject, for the purpose of astonishing your hearers with your erudition." There were ways to conceal aesthetic ignorance. Faced with an incomprehensible work of art, "you can always say that it is 'very intellectual,' 'very strong,' or 'very profound'—but never 'charming,' " instructs one etiquette writer. Alas, the authors could offer no help for when the commissioned portrait was unveiled. But be wary, one book cautions: "[T]hese famous painters generally interpret what they see in a most original manner, and while it may be charming in a still life or a landscape, it is a bit disconcerting to see your own head transformed into a ripe pear or a coffeepot."

"It is an irksome task to show any sort of picture to people who have neither taste, knowledge, nor enjoyment of the art. There are persons (ungenteel ones, it is true) who seem to have no other pleasure, when looking at a fine print or picture, than in trying to discover in the figures or faces, fancied resemblances to those of some individuals of their own circle: loudly declaring for instance, that, 'Queen Victoria is the very image of Sarah Smith'; 'Prince Albert an exact likeness of Dick Brown'; 'the Duke of Wellington the very ditto of old Captain Jones,' &c.&c. To those 'who have no painting in their souls,' there is little use in showing or explaining any fine specimen of that noblest of the fine arts."

MISS LESLIE'S BEHAVIOUR BOOK
Miss Leslie, 1859

"On the other hand, the best society will not endure dilettantism, and whatever the knowledge a man may possess of any art, he must not display it so as to make the ignorance of others painful to them. We are gentlemen, not picture-dealers."

THE HABITS OF GOOD SOCIETY
Anonymous, 1859

"What is one of the most common errors people make when speaking to a writer?"

The woman who goes up to the writer at a cocktail party and tells him how she has always wanted to write but just hasn't had the time, as though it were as simple as making a hairdresser appointment. . . . Also the person who asks, 'Is it true that everyone has a book in him?' Normally, the writer is polite and mutters something nice and then must stand on one foot and then another with a hot martini and soggy onion listening to her life story."

PRACTICAL ETIQUETTE FOR THE MODERN MAN
Mary Lou Munson, 1964

• • •

"It was well said by a late eminent barrister, that literature in ladies should be what onions ought to be in cookery; you should perceive the flavour, but not detect the thing itself."

THE HABITS OF GOOD SOCIETY
Anonymous, 1859

"Never tell an authoress that 'you are afraid of her'—or entreat her 'not to put you into a book.' Be assured there is no danger."

MISS LESLIE'S BEHAVIOUR BOOK
Miss Leslie, 1859

THE PERFECT LAUGH

"To laugh aloud is a dangerous thing . . ." warns the author of an etiquette book. Laughter exposed one's background as indisputably as the way one spoke. "The ruder the people are, the louder and coarser will be their expressions of enjoyment," reveals a writer.

The truly refined made no noise at all. "In my mind, there is nothing so illiberal, and so ill-bred, as audible laughter," observes Lord Chesterfield, who deemed it "the mirth of the mob." "A man of parts and fashion is therefore only seen to smile, but never heard to laugh," he contends.

A colleague disagrees: "There is no greater ornament to conversation than the ripple of silvery notes that forms the perfect laugh." The only problem was the imperfect laugh. Not to worry, she assures us: Laughter could be taught as successfully as a series of elocution lessons. "The only thing to be guarded against is that the inculcated laugh is apt to grow stereotyped," she concedes, "and few things are more irritating than to hear it over and over again, begin on the same note, run down the same scale, and consequently express no more mirth than the keys of the piano."

"Never cackle or shriek."

ETIQUETTE FOR AMERICANS
By a Woman of Fashion, 1909

"The person who snorts when she laughs is also out of order."

MANNERS FOR MILLIONS
Sophie C. Hadida, 1932

"Immoderate laughter is exceedingly unbecoming in a lady; she may affect the dimple or the smile, but should carefully avoid any approximation to a horse-laugh."

THE PERFECT GENTLEMAN
By a Gentleman, 1860

"The prudery which sits in solemn and severe rebuke at a *double entendre* is only second in indelicacy to the indecency which grows hilarious over it, since both must recognize the evil intent. . . . A lady will always fail to hear that which she should not hear, or, having unmistakably heard, she will not understand."

DECORUM
Anonymous, 1877

"A lady-punster is a most unpleasing phenomenon, and we would advise no young woman, however witty she may be, to cultivate this kind of verbal talent."

COLLIER'S CYCLOPEDIA OF COMMERCIAL AND SOCIAL INFORMATION
Compiled by Nugent Robinson, 1882

"A wit is a very unpopular denomination, as it carries terror along with it; and people in general are as much afraid of a live wit, in company, as a woman is of a gun, which she thinks may go off of itself, and do her a mischief."

LETTERS TO HIS SON
The Earl of Chesterfield, 1748; 1937

•　　•　　•

"Avoid raillery and sarcasm in social parties. They are weapons which few can use; and because you happen to have a razor in your possession, that is no reason why you should be allowed to cut the throats of the rest who are unarmed."

THE LADY'S BOOK OF MANNERS
Anonymous, 1870

"Furthermore, it is not right to say or do anything cheap or unseemly, such as pulling faces and striking poses, in order to make other people laugh, for no one should debase himself to please others, which is the trade of clowns and jesters not of dignified persons. You must not therefore . . . pretend to be insane or eccentric."

GALATEO *OR* THE BOOK OF MANNERS
Giovanni Della Casa, 1558; translated by R. S. Pine-Coffin, 1958

"And, unless you cannot control your enjoyment of your wit, do not laugh or chuckle over your own jokes—to do so is as if you should stop and clap your hands at what you think one of your eloquent passages."

THE ART OF PUBLIC SPEAKING
Albert J. Beveridge, 1924

Chapter 7

MANNERS
FOR HOSTS
AND HOUSEGUESTS

And Other Weekend Frolickers

THE COUNTRY WEEKEND

"My dear Mrs. Pickling," the hostess of a country house might write, "It will give me great pleasure if you and Mr. Pickling will come to us Friday afternoon and remain until the Monday noon train. Stoddard will meet you at the station at four thirty. Your train leaves the city at two."

In America, Stoddard might be surprised by an entourage of servants stepping off the train with the Picklings, but in England it was taken for granted that an invitation to a lady included her personal maid as well, bearing the jewel-case, while the valet struggled with his lordship's trunk.

A stroll to the stables or the kennels, or a turn around the garden might follow greetings upon the veranda, but a proud hostess was cautioned: "When showing off your own garden, avoid doing . . . a sudden breathless halt and clasping of hands when a tuft of thrift has flowered again. They do not know it was not expected to flower again." Mr. and Mrs. Pickling were also advised: "Avoid, in the same way, saying to the hostess, when looking at her autumn crocuses, or something even rarer, like her fritillaries: 'Ours grow like weeds.'"

After an evening of charades, dancing, cards, moonlit skating, or séances, the weary Picklings were handed candles to navigate their way through darkened corridors to the guest room. This chamber could be either heaven or hell, depending upon the thoughtfulness of the hostess. If the Picklings were greeted with a tin of biscuits and a thermos of tea beside the bed; a hot water bottle hanging over the door; wedges of either wood or brass suspended by chains alongside the window frames to silence rattling glass; working bells to summon the servants; reading material "chosen more to divert than to engross" (and please, not just last year's seed catalogue! protests one writer); new cakes of scented and unscented soap, violet water, bath salts, hairbrush, hat brush, clothes brush, shoehorns, buttonhooks, pomade, perfume; and stamps, stationery, ink, blotting paper, and telegraph blanks; then the satisfied guests would know that they were under the roof of a considerate hostess and that she had probably, at some time (as many etiquette authors recommended), spent an entire night in this room pretending to be the Picklings in their every need.

In the morning, Mrs. Pickling might be wakened by the crackling of a fire prepared while she slept, or by the maid, knocking at the door, bearing a breakfast tray laden with china chosen to match the decor of the room and a newspaper chosen to match the politics of its occupant, as well as any letters that might have arrived in the morning post. This luxury would occur only if Mrs. Pickling had filled out the following form the night before (Mr. Pickling, it was assumed, would be up and out early with the other male members of the shooting party):

PLEASE FILL THIS OUT BEFORE GOING DOWN TO DINNER:
What time do you want to be awakened?_____
Or, will you ring?_____
Will you breakfast upstairs?_____
Or down?_____

UNDERSCORE YOUR ORDERS:
Coffee, tea, chocolate, milk,

"In visiting a friend for a short stay
never take a trunk so big that it suggests the possibility
of an indefinite lingering."

Oatmeal, hominy, shredded wheat,
Eggs, how cooked?
Rolls, muffins, toast,
Orange, pear, grapes, melon.

The schedule of country house visiting left mornings free, the host and hostess to attend to their business and domestic affairs, Mrs. Pickling to remain in her room writing letters and reading novels, or gossiping out on the veranda. Around midday, the entire company would gather together and a guest was expected to join in enthusiastically, no matter what the agenda. "If you go for a drive, and it pours, and there is no top to the carriage or car, and you are soaked to the skin and chilled to the marrow so that your teeth chatter, your lips must smile and you must appear to enjoy the refreshing coolness," instructs Emily Post. If you are really miserable, she adds, you can walk to the neighboring village and send yourself a telegram demanding your presence back at home.

But the wise guest learned to enjoy, even to savor, every moment away from home: "Light all the candles: they are meant to be lit," advises one author. "Don't behave as you do at home, sparing your light, your soap and your towel, but wash and wash, and light up—that is the way to be a good guest. Be lavish, for to-morrow we die."

"In visiting a friend for a short stay never take a trunk so big that it suggests the possibility of an indefinite lingering."

GOOD MANNERS FOR ALL OCCASIONS
Margaret E. Sangster, 1921

"The horrors of the guest room are too well known to need enumeration, and can seldom be ameliorated. They are, roughly, as follows: The embroidered pillow slips, the egg-finished sheets, the drawer of the bureau that is warped and will not open, the rusty pins in the stony pincushion, the empty cut-glass cologne bottles, the blinds that bang in the night, the absence of hooks on which to hang your razor strop, the pictures of the 'Huguenot Lovers' and Landseer's 'Sanctuary' over the headboard of the bed, the tendency of the maid to hide the matches, the dear little children in the nursery above you, the dead fly in the dried-up ink well, and the hidden radiator under the sofa."

MANNERS FOR THE METROPOLIS
Francis W. Crowninshield, 1909

"No house should be without its guest-chamber. Besides giving one's home an air of hospitality, it makes an admirable store-room for dilapidated furniture and unspeakable pictures."

THE CYNIC'S RULES OF CONDUCT
Chester Field, Jr., 1905

"The passage through a country house of the framed photograph of a friend is often an instructive spectacle to witness. Such a trophy usually begins its career in the drawing-room. It is then moved to the library, and subsequently to the smoking room. After that it begins a heavenly flight into one of the guest rooms, from which place it ascends on its last earthly pilgrimage to the attic."

MANNERS FOR THE METROPOLIS
Francis W. Crowninshield, 1909

"Pictures should never be hung so high that it becomes necessary to mount a chair in order to see them."

A BACHELOR'S CUPBOARD
A. Lyman Phillips, 1906

"[T]he modern hostess would no more venture to ask two women just introduced to one another to occupy the same bed, than she would dare to provide them with but one plate at her table."

ENCYCLOPAEDIA OF ETIQUETTE
Emily Holt, 1901

"Certain bodily effluvia are thrown off from our persons, and where two individuals sleep together each inhales from the other more or less of these emanations. . . . When not practicable for individuals to occupy separate beds, the persons should be of about the same age, and in good health. Numerous cases have occurred where healthy, robust children, have '*dwindled away*' and died within a few months, from sleeping with old people."

THE PEOPLE'S COMMON SENSE MEDICAL ADVISER
R. V. Pierce, 1876

"A well-made bed is one of the greatest joys man knows."

THE HOW AND WHY OF HOME ETIQUETTE
Josephine Perry, 1934

"Nothing is more tortuous than to slowly perish with chill in a strange house."

COURTESY BOOK
Horace J. Gardner and Patricia Farren, 1937

"Shut doors quietly. There are people whose nerves are so sensitive that doors slammed to will almost make them ill."

TWENTIETH CENTURY ETIQUETTE
Annie Randall White, 1900

"In hot weather, every guest should have a palm leaf fan . . ."

ETIQUETTE
Emily Post, 1922

"To listen at door cracks and peep through key holes is vulgar and contemptible."

THE STANDARD CYCLOPAEDIA OF USEFUL KNOWLEDGE, vol. V
Anonymous, 1896

•　　•　　•

"Pictures should never be hung so high that it becomes
necessary to mount a chair in order to see them."

"To permit children to ask visiters for pennies or sixpences is mean and contemptible."

MISS LESLIE'S BEHAVIOUR BOOK
Miss Leslie, 1859

"A gentleman visitor who neither shoots, fishes, boats, reads, writes letters, nor does anything but hang about, letting himself be 'amused,' is an intolerable nuisance. He had better go to the billiard-room and practice caroms by himself, or retire to the stables and smoke."

MANNERS AND SOCIAL USAGES
Mrs. John Sherwood, 1897

"To invite a friend to one's house and then seem to find her presence unwelcome is only a degree less cruel than confining a bird in a cage, where he cannot forage for himself, and slowly starving him."

PRESENT DAY ETIQUETTE
Virginia Van de Water, 1936

"In other days, when slow traveling made distance distressingly fatiguing, no limit was set upon a guest's visit. In fact, one young woman who went to spend a fortnight with friends in Virginia stayed thirty years—until she died."

ETIQUETTE
Emily Post, 1942

PEN PALS

A foresighted houseguest packed a small writing case furnished with ink, stationery, and stamps, for country mornings were often spent in the leisurely pastime of letter writing. As dramatic as the local falls were, guests were not to send a postcard of the view. "People of good taste do not use postcards for social correspondence of any kind," declares an etiquette writer, and so insulting was this exposed correspondence that some authors considered it "questionable whether a note on a postal-card is entitled to the courtesy of a response."

Tucked away in an envelope, a letter may be free from the curious eyes of the postman, but the author was not yet free from the scrutiny of etiquette. "The lesser niceties of folding, sealing, and superscription, are not beneath the notice of a lady," observes a writer. Even the placement of the postage stamp did not go unnoted, particularly since it "has been invested with a language of its own," reveals a writer in 1908. "When the stamp is in the center at the top it signifies an affirmative answer to a question . . . and when it is at the bottom, it is a negative," he decodes. "Should the stamp be on the right-hand corner, at a right angle, it asks the question if the receiver of the letter loves the sender; while in the left-hand corner means that the writer hates the other." Such whimsy was shocking, scowl the etiquette writers: "It looks very slovenly and careless to see a stamp put on to an envelope in an unusual place, or in a crooked and irregular way. Little things like these always attract attention, and create an unfavorable impression."

Finally, it was forbidden to close with a seal. "[W]e must use sealing wax. Men usually select red," observes a woman in 1886, "but young ladies use gilt, rose, and other colors. Both use black wax when they are in mourning." Care should be paid to the destination, however, before applying the wax: "In a foreign correspondence, the self-sealing envelopes are better since in tropical countries the great heat often melts the wax . . . during transportation in the holds of vessels . . ." causing letters to become "irretrievably glued together, to the loss of the address and the confusion of the postmaster."

"It is as rude to leave a letter unanswered as it is to leave a question unanswered in conversation."

MANNERS FOR GIRLS
Mrs. Humphry, 1901

•   •   •

"Letters reeking with a supposedly pleasant odor are the hallmarks of the cheap women affecting smartness. The true lady never scents her letters."

THE NEW AMERICAN ETIQUETTE
Edited by Lily Haxworth Wallace, 1941

"Of course none but country lads and lasses ever use red or blue inks."

OUR MANNERS AND SOCIAL CUSTOMS
Daphne Dale, 1891

"Pallid inks, faint and elusive, are abominations."

GOOD MANNERS FOR ALL OCCASIONS
Margaret E. Sangster, 1921

"Notepaper with a dainty flower in one corner is as much out of place in the writing-desk of the middle aged as a flowery hat would be upon her head."

MANNERS FOR GIRLS
Mrs. Humphry, 1901

"Severe plainness is always elegant."

WESTERN ETIQUETTE
Annina Periam Danton, 1929

"In writing to a person much your superior or inferior, use as few words as possible. In the former case, to take up much of a great man's time is to take a liberty; in the latter, to be diffuse is to be too familiar."

THE STANDARD CYCLOPAEDIA OF USEFUL KNOWLEDGE, vol. V
Anonymous, 1896

"In writing to persons decidedly your inferiors in station, avoid the probability of mortifying them by sending mean, ill-looking notes."

MISS LESLIE'S BEHAVIOUR BOOK
Miss Leslie, 1859

*"Nothing can be more absurd than to see a person whose name
can have no significance to the world in general, sign himself
as elaborately as if he were the Pope or President at least."*

"Never send a letter with a blot on it."

ETIQUETTE
Emily Post, 1922

"The clerkly hand is not one to be cultivated for ordinary correspondence, since it is too suggestive of boxes and bales, or dry as dust parchments and papers."

OUR MANNERS AND SOCIAL CUSTOMS
Daphne Dale, 1891

"Never attempt to convey the impression that you are a genius, by imitating the faults of distinguished men. Because certain great men were poor penmen, wore long hair, or had other peculiarities, it does not follow that you will be great by imitating their eccentricities."

HILL'S MANUAL OF SOCIAL AND BUSINESS FORMS
Thos. E. Hill, 1882

"Nothing can be more absurd than to see a person whose name can have no significance to the world in general, sign himself as elaborately as if he were the Pope or President at least."

FROST'S LAWS AND BY-LAWS OF AMERICAN SOCIETY
S. A. Frost, 1869

"[U]se as few parentheses as possible; it is a clumsy way of disposing of a sentence, and often embarrasses the reader."

THE LADY'S GUIDE TO COMPLETE ETIQUETTE
Emily Thornwell, 1886

"Lady correspondents are too apt to emphasize in their letter writing, and in general evince a sad disregard of the laws of punctuation. We would respectfully suggest that a comma is not designed to answer every purpose, and that the underlining of every second or third word adds nothing to the eloquence or clearness of a letter, however certain it may be to provoke an unflattering smile upon the lips of the reader."

THE STANDARD CYCLOPAEDIA OF USEFUL KNOWLEDGE, vol. V
Anonymous, 1896

"Very dainty young ladies affect a pink tinted paper and violet perfumed ink, upon which basis they begin a gushing correspondence with six or eight school friends, wherein the adjectives suffer much harm."

GEMS OF DEPORTMENT
Anonymous, 1880

"I have seen a pretty young woman, while writing a letter to her lover, draw up her lips, and twist the muscles of her face in every direction that her pen moved; and so ugly did she look during this sympathetic performance, that I could not forbear thinking that, could her swain see the object then dictating her vows, he would take fright at the metamorphosis, and never be made to believe it could be the same person."

THE LADIES' HAND-BOOK OF ETIQUETTE
Anonymous, ca. 1867

"[A] lady should not write to a man if she can avoid it. And girls, above all, should, of course, do so as seldom as they possibly can. All men are not gentlemen, thick and glossy as their veneer may be; and many a man has shown the effusive epistle of a love-sick maiden, long after she has loathed the object to whom it was penned."

ETIQUETTE FOR AMERICANS
By a Woman of Fashion, 1909

"If you are late with a letter, don't apologize so much it makes it seem that having to write is just the final straw on top of everything else that's happened to you."

ETIQUETTE ETC.
Sheila Ostrander, 1967

"Do not amass a previous store of brilliant or profound ideas in order to dispose of them in your letters as occasion may require. In the epistolary style, it is especially true, that we must live from day to day."

ETIQUETTE OF TO-DAY
John Wesley Hanson, Jr., 1896

"Never send a letter which has produced weariness or trouble in writing. It would certainly weary the reader."

ETIQUETTE OF TO-DAY
John Wesley Hanson, Jr., 1896

"Above all, never send an inquiry or compliment in a postscript. . . . Nobody likes to see their name mentioned as an afterthought."

THE LADIES' BOOK OF ETIQUETTE, AND MANUAL OF POLITENESS
Florence Hartley, 1873

"Don't fasten an envelope by moistening the mucilage with your lips; but this custom is too universally established for a protest against it to be of much avail. No one, however, can defend the practice as altogether nice."

DON'TS FOR EVERYBODY
Compiled by Frederic Reddale, 1907

"Sending out a letter with a crooked, mangled, or upside-down stamp is akin to letting your lingerie straps show."

GOOD HOUSEKEEPING'S BOOK OF TODAY'S ETIQUETTE
Louise Raymond, 1965

BOOKWORMS

The houseguest who could not tear herself away from her room in the morning may not have been absorbed in the profundities of the Bible but in the titillations of the latest novel. "A glance at the plots of some of the most popular novels of the day . . ." preaches the Reverend Dix in an 1878 etiquette book, "demonstrate that to be quiet, decent, and mannerly, is to be stupid and dull; that if you wish to be thought interesting and brilliant, you must be fast and free; that it is natural and right to do the meanest and most odious things. . . . The result of all this," he concludes, "is unfortunately too plain and most evident in the manners of the young women of the period."

But the long-term effects of novel reading were much greater than a simple loss of propriety in the drawing room. "Novel-reading has led thousands to lives of dissoluteness," discloses a writer. "The result is, that through the reading of exciting novels, they fall into habits of self-indulgence and abuse," explains another author, who proceeds to narrate the downward path of one bookworm: "In one seminary where I lectured, a girl had found her way to the lunatic asylum through lying in bed until two and three o'clock in the morning reading novels. The principal had upbraided her several times for not having her lessons, but she grew worse and worse until her father was finally sent for to take her home, and from there she went to the insane asylum."

With such consequences at stake, several etiquette authors took it upon themselves to suggest a more prodigious reading list. But one was wiser: "We will not say to them, as some advisers would, throw all your novels in the fire, and set yourself resolutely about reading Gibbon's 'Rome' or Hume's 'England' " for "we are sure the readers of whom we are speaking will never make the transition from 'The Pioneer's Daughter' or 'The Missing Bride' to Gibbon and Hume." Try instead to switch to fictional works of travel and adventure, and perhaps "the reading of these may readily be made to introduce more solid works." But the transition will not be easy, predicts another: "A confirmed novel-reader is almost as difficult to reform as a confirmed inebriate or opium-eater."

"No young man or young woman can afford to read fiction before they are twenty-five years of age."

WHAT A YOUNG MAN OUGHT TO KNOW
Sylvanus Stall, 1904

"It may be well to remind our sentimental readers that all unnecessary weeping had better be avoided, for the delights of crying over the jilted Augustus or the broken-hearted Araminta of the last novel can not be indulged in without risk to the health and beauty of the eyes."

THE BAZAR BOOK OF DECORUM
Anonymous, 1870

"Of course, you know that it is wrong to lick your fingers when turning over the pages of a book."

THINGS THAT ARE NOT DONE
Edgar and Diana Woods, 1937

"Should you have contagious disease in your family, you should not take books from the library until the patient recovers, even though the patient is in isolation from the household. Germs are often so minute as to be imperceptible, and germs may easily find lodgment between the leaves of a book, and weeks or months afterward convey the seed of fever and perhaps carry death to people whom you do not know."

GOOD MANNERS FOR ALL OCCASIONS
Margaret E. Sangster, 1921

"Return a borrowed book, when you have finished reading it, without delay. A library made up of borrowed books is a disgraceful possession."

OUR HOME
C. E. Sargent, 1883

• • •

"Don't try to get your opponent's eye off the ball by antics like brandishing your racket in the midst of his stroke."

"Some valuable books when they come back to their too kindly owner present the appearance of having been used as a portable dinner-table, the once unsullied pages wearing the aspect of a greasy table-cloth. This is vulgar and indecent, but even worse than this is it to find one's book desecrated by the idiotic remarks and egotistic emendations of the conceited coxcomb, or, let us charitably hope, silly lunatic, to whom in a moment of amiable weakness we lent the cherished volume which had solaced many a lonely and enlivened many a leisure hour. The shock is almost as great as if we saw again the face of a dear friend besmeared with mud by some miserable urchin of the gutter. Nothing has ever made a rational being regret his ability to read so much as the perusal of these inane, asinine comments and presumed improvements on some favorite author, written on the margin. Show us the girl who cannot admire a sentence or a sentiment without scrawling 'very true' or 'how beautiful' beside it, and we will show you a girl whom the sensible young men of her neighborhood will do well to avoid. No rational man would make love or offer marriage to one of these feminine annotators. She would write her impressions on his shirt front and make remarks upon his cuffs."

THE HEARTHSTONE; OR, LIFE AT HOME
Laura C. Holloway, 1883

"Don't sit around and read lovey-dovey novels or spend your time chatting with that stupid woman next door. Don't forget that life is short and there's not a moment to waste."

THE NEW CENTURY PERFECT SPEAKER
Edited by John Coulter, 1901

A GOOD SPORT

Hunting was a man's sport, but "[u]nless you are a hopeless misogynist you won't in the least mind a party of ladies coming out to lunch with you and eating, with merriment, from the goodly spread of mutton and pigeon pies, cold meats, sausage rolls and even hot Irish stew!" exclaims an author.

While the viands were often transported to the scene under the fastidious care of servants, these helpers were to vanish when their masters were "gypsying by the wooded stream," commands an etiquette authority. "[N]othing is more justly ridiculous than that people who come out to play the rustic should be accompanied by . . . some half-dozen stately acolytes of fashion moving about us with all the solemnity of a London dinner-party."

Gentlemen were to play the role of servants, watching and waiting to meet every woman's need. If the ladies desire nuts, the gentlemen were the ones to climb the trees, shake the limbs, and carry the nuts back to their companions. "Gentlemen at pic-nics must consent to become waiters, guides, servants to the ladies; must 'scale mountains,' climb trees, perform any feats desired by the fair tyrants, if they fancy 'that lovely flower,' or 'exquisite bunch of sea-weed,' in impossible-to-get-at places," maintains a writer.

As gallant as the gentlemen may be, they failed promptly if they spread the cloth out of relief of the shade, for "it is impossible to hold up a parasol during luncheon . . ." one writer notes. The sensitive nerves of the fair guests should also be considered when selecting the site: "One does not feel too comfortable when banquetting in localities where Dame Nature has had her queer moods, and has left imprinted certain too observable evidences of her freakiness," observes a writer. "Such places may be included within the excursion itself, but let the feast and the frolic take place where weird effects are not the prevailing characteristic of the locality." "Care should also be taken to see that the guests are not seated upon an ant-hill . . ." adds another.

The meal over, the women often loitered in their leave-taking, to the great annoyance of the gentlemen, who were eager to "resume their work of destruction." "If only the women will have the sense to go off in decent time," one man complains, but "*They often do not,* and then the fly in the ointment is a very large one."

Sometimes women accompanied the men for the remainder of the day, watching, of course, from a respectful distance. It was imperative to dress sensibly for this excursion, as it was absurd to see a woman trailing behind a party of marksmen in the latest Paris fashions. "It is hardly necessary to add that petticoats are *never* worn on the moors . . ." frowns an author. "A pleated skirt is useful," she advises, "though perhaps one which buttons up the side is best, as it is then possible to unfasten it when there is a hedge to be negotiated or some other obstacle."

Whether the object of the hunt was fox, hare, grouse, partridge, pheasant or waterfowl, certain courtesies of the field were to be observed. "If you are sitting in a blind and the ducks swoop down to the water and sit there, do not shoot," orders an etiquette writer. "You are only permitted to shoot when they take off again, and you should give them time to gather momentum and gain a fair speed before taking aim at them. And *never* shoot into a flock of birds with the hope that you might drop one."

At the hunt's end "[t]he party rides back in leisurely fashion and are awaited by the rest of the house-party with gathering interest. The story of the run is recounted and the day ends its pleasant course." But the reclusive houseguest who stayed behind reading and writing letters in her room was not to inquire if the party had "a good day's hunting" but rather "a good run." "And never refer to hounds as 'dogs,' " one author pleads.

"A man who wears a red coat to hunt in, should be able to hunt, and not sneak through gates or dodge over gaps."

THE HABITS OF GOOD SOCIETY
Anonymous, 1859

"If you are walking with a woman in the country,—ascending a mountain or strolling by the bank of a river,—and your companion being fatigued, should choose to sit upon the ground, on no account allow yourself to do the same, but remain rigorously standing. To do otherwise would be flagrantly indecorous and she would probably resent it as the greatest insult."

DECORUM
Anonymous, 1877

• • •

"A silk hat should only be worn on appropriate occasions. Worn with a rough business suit, or on a picnic or mountain ramble, it is in the worst possible taste."

SOCIAL ETIQUETTE
Maud C. Cooke, 18—

"White furs should only be worn by experienced skaters, for they easily become soiled by the novitiate in tumbles upon the ice."

THE LADIES' AND GENTLEMEN'S ETIQUETTE
Mrs. E. B. Duffey, 1877

"To play cards with an air of weariness or abstraction is positively rude. If you are not interested in the game, strive to appear so, and if you are not equal to that, you had better stop playing."

FROST'S LAWS AND BY-LAWS OF AMERICAN SOCIETY
S. A. Frost, 1869

"Do not whistle when playing cards. You may blow the other fellow's cards out of his hand."

MANNERS FOR MILLIONS
Sophie C. Hadida, 1932

"Slapping and waving the cards is a source of irritation to those who are losing; gentlemen do not intentionally nettle the unfortunate."

THE BOOK OF GOOD MANNERS
Victor H. Diescher, 1923

"Don't try to get your opponent's eye off the ball by antics like brandishing your racket in the midst of his stroke."

THE CORRECT THING
William Oliver Stevens, 1934

• • •

"Criticising another's play is almost as bad as criticising his clothes."

THE BOOK OF GOOD MANNERS
Victor H. Diescher, 1923

"To stop in the middle of a match that seems lost, complaining of an injury that existed before you started, is to court unfavorable criticism."

THE BOOK OF GOOD MANNERS
Victor H. Diescher, 1923

"When you leave off playing, converse with your adversary, and not seem to avoid him but be careful never to speak to him of his good luck in playing unless it be with a frank gaiety, otherwise you would seem to be inspired with anger."

THE GENTLEMAN AND LADY'S BOOK OF POLITENESS
Mme. Celnart, 1835

"One last and earnestly urged 'Don't' is the loser's practise of complaining of illness after having lost a match. This is one real flaw in the average woman's sportsmanship."

ETIQUETTE
Emily Post, 1942

BACK ROADS

Should two houseguests slip out for a ride down a lonely country road, it was wisest to select the stable's drabbest mares over its finest carriage, for etiquette required the chaperonage of a chauffeur or footman on such an excursion and in a horse-drawn vehicle "no matter how fast you drive you cannot shake him off; but in the saddle, a brisk trot or a sharp canter will leave James at a judicious distance in the rear, especially if he has been provided with a good, slow nag." An avid equestrienne might dress for this rendezvous in a skirt with shot sewn into the hem to prevent the material from blowing upwards and exposing a leg.

*"If the lady be light, you must take care not
to give her too much impetus in mounting."*

James's service was just as necessary when she mounted a bicycle, but with this vehicle his presence became as indiscreet as an umbilical cord. "Very gallant escorts use a towrope when accompanying a lady on a wheeling spin," explains an author. "One end is attached to the lady's wheel at the lamp bracket or brake rod by a spring swivel, and the other end is hooked to the escort's handle bar. . . . When he has finished towing he drops back to the lady's side, hanging the loose end of the cord over her shoulder, to be ready for the next hill."

But when she propelled herself, the well-bred wheelwoman never pedaled so hard that she panted. "The 'uneducated mouth' is one of the indications of bad breeding," reveals a writer. Nor did she improvise a tune on her bicycle's bell, "that will do for the vulgar herd who delight in noise." The wide-open skies do not free a cyclist from the constraints of decorum. "A lady can be as reserved upon a wheel as in her parlor," one writer proclaims.

"Never appear in public on horseback unless you have mastered the inelegancies attending a first appearance in the saddle."

DECORUM
Anonymous, 1877

"If the lady be light, you must take care not to give her too much impetus in mounting. We have known a lady nearly thrown over her horse by a misplaced zeal of this kind."

COLLIER'S CYCLOPEDIA OF COMMERCIAL AND SOCIAL INFORMATION
Compiled by Nugent Robinson, 1882

"A lady who has a secure seat is never prettier than when in the saddle, and she who cannot make her conquests there, may despair of the power of her charms elsewhere."

THE MANNERS THAT WIN
Anonymous, 1880

"In riding with a lady, never permit her to pay the tolls."

THE STANDARD CYCLOPAEDIA OF USEFUL KNOWLEDGE, vol. V
Anonymous, 1896

"On the road, the constant care of the gentleman should be to render the ride agreeable to his companion, by the pointing out of objects of interest with which she may not be acquainted, the reference to any peculiar beauty of landscape which may have escaped her notice, and a general lively tone of conversation, which will, if she be timid, draw her mind from the fancied dangers of horseback riding, and render her excursion much more agreeable than if she be left to imagine horrors whenever her horse may prick up his ears or whisk his tail."

THE GENTLEMEN'S BOOK OF ETIQUETTE AND MANUAL OF POLITENESS
Cecil B. Hartley, 1860

"[I]t is bad manners, when you see something to nauseate you by the roadside, as sometimes happens, to turn to your companions and point it out to them. Still less should you offer any evil smelling object for others to sniff, as some people do, insisting upon holding it up to their noses and asking them to smell how horrible it is."

GALATEO *OR* THE BOOK OF MANNERS
Giovanni Della Casa, 1558; translated by R. S. Pine-Coffin, 1958

"Don't go out on a bicycle wearing a tail coat unless you enjoy making a ridiculous show of yourself."

SOCIAL ETIQUETTE
Maud C. Cooke, 18—

"Don't ride ten miles at a scorching pace, then drink cold water and lie around on the grass, unless you are tired of life."

SOCIAL ETIQUETTE
Maud C. Cooke, 18—

"I consider the bicycle rider by moonlight a dangerous enemy to the human race . . ."

MANNERS AND SOCIAL USAGES
Mrs. John Sherwood, 1897

SUNDAY SERVICE

With the turn of the century came a change in attitude toward church on the part of the "smart set," reports an etiquette writer in 1906. Among certain opulent circles "may be noticed the prevalence of divorce, the ultra style of dress, the immoderate playing of bridge whist and other games of chance for high stakes, the prevalence of excessive drinking among women, Sunday golfing, automobiling and yachting, and Sunday house-parties *sans* church, although as a matter of form a conveyance is provided for such few guests as may desire to attend church, because it would not be 'English' to make such an omission."

But the provision of a carriage may have been an act of blasphemy in itself, for true believers shunned all displays of fortune when frequenting places of worship. "The newly rich people, after the service, although their homes may be only a few blocks distant from the church, will, of course, betake themselves to their carriages like religious cripples," sneers an author, but when distance permits, "people of breeding and true refinement *walk* to church."

When the minister came to call, hostesses were instructed to watch their food. "Our most profound disgust is justly excited when we hear of laxity of morals in a clergyman," preaches an author. "But when we consider how these ministers are fed, we cannot suppress a momentary disposition to excuse, in some degree, their fault."

"Any disturbance of the digestive function deteriorates the quality of the blood," he explains. "Poor blood, filled with crude, poorly digested food, is irritating to the nervous system, and especially to those extremely delicate nerves which govern the reproductive function. Irritation provokes congestion; congestion excites sexual desires; excited passions increase the local disturbance; and thus each reacts upon the other. . . .

"When the minister goes out to tea, he is served with the richest cake, the choicest jellies, the most pungent sauces, and the finest of fine-flour bread-stuffs. Little does the indulgent hostess dream that she is ministering to the in-flammation of passions which may imperil the virtue of her daughter, or even her own. Salacity once aroused, even in a minister, allows no room for reason or for conscience. If women wish to preserve the virtue of their ministers, let them feed them more in accordance with the laws of health. Ministers are not immaculate."

"Don't absent yourself from church to go wheeling, as you and your bicycle are welcome at most houses of worship."

SOCIAL ETIQUETTE
Maud C. Cooke, 18—

"True Christian courtesy will naturally dictate that you share your pew with the stranger within your gates. I once saw a woman at Newport make a great fuss over a gentlewoman's being ushered, at the proper time, too, into the pew which she was occupying in solitary state. I looked up that pew-holder's antecedents and learned that one of her forefathers had been a very coarse butcher."

CORRECT SOCIAL USAGE, vol. I
Rev. C. W. de Lyon Nichols, et al., 1906

"Do not fan violently in church."

SOCIAL CONDUCT
The Church of Jesus Christ of Latter-day Saints, 1934

•   •   •

"All nodding, whispering, and exchanging of glances in church, is in bad taste. Even the latter should not be indulged in, unless a very charming woman is the provoking cause of the peccadillo, and then very stealthily and circumspectly!"

THE AMERICAN GENTLEMAN'S GUIDE TO POLITENESS AND FASHION
Henry Lunettes, 1863

"The church is not the proper place to conduct a courtship . . ."

SEARCH LIGHTS ON HEALTH
Prof. B. G. Jefferis and J. L. Nichols, 1896

"Never eat lozenges or peppermints in church."

GOOD MANNERS FOR ALL OCCASIONS
Margaret E. Sangster, 1921

"Nor is it proper to read a paper or book during the service, as it appears disrespectful to the minister, the choir, and the congregation, by an implied indifference to the sermon and the services."

GOOD MORALS AND GENTLE MANNERS
Alex M. Gow, 1873

"The singing of the choir may be good; if so, one should not listen to it with the air of a *connoisseur* at a grand concert. Or the singing may be very poor; that fact should not be emphasized by the scowling countenance of the critic in the pews."

ETIQUETTE
Agnes H. Morton, 1892

"Applause is out of order at any religious service."

YOUR BEST FOOT FORWARD
Dorothy C. Stratton and Helen B. Schleman, 1955

DEPARTING GUESTS

As the hour for parting neared, a hostess's relief at the departure of her guests was not to be indulged in until after they were gone. The final adieu was to be performed with the same hospitality as the first hello.

"Go with them to the depot. Treat them with such kindness and cordiality to the close that recollection of their visit will ever be a bright spot in their memory. Remain with them until the train arrives. They would be very lonely waiting without you. You will ever remember with pleasure the fact that you made the last hours of their visit pleasant. And thus, with the last hand-shaking, and the last waving of adieu, as the train speeds away, keep up the warmth of hospitality with your guests to the very end. It is, perhaps, the last time you will ever see them."

HILL'S MANUAL OF SOCIAL AND BUSINESS FORMS
Thos. E. Hill, 1882

Chapter 8

MANNERS FOR COMMUTERS AND CLERKS

And Other City Promenaders

THE DAILY GRIND

As the nineteenth century rolled into the twentieth, a new creature emerged from the dark and velveted parlor and stood blinking on the bright city sidewalks: the Working Woman. She threw the etiquette book authors into a tizzy. Some desperately tried to straddle both worlds, the past and the present. Nowhere did this double standard reveal itself better than under the subject of chaperons. "As a business woman, the self-reliant young girl does not need a chaperone," instructs one author. "The spectacle of a stately middle-aged woman accompanying each girl book-keeper to her desk every morning would be burlesque in the extreme." But released from the purpose of work and seeking relaxation, "[a]s a society woman, this inexperienced, sensitive, human-nature-trusting child *does* need a chaperone. She is, therefore, subject to what we may call intermittent chaperonage."

Confusions began to arise. The rule that "a young girl must never go to a restaurant with a young man unless a chaperon accompanies them" and the instruction "[n]o young girl ought to let herself in with a latch-key" began to grow cumbersome. Was the working girl to have her chaperon unlock her front door as she emerged from the rush-hour subway? And did the lunch that fell in the middle of a workday fall under the category of business or social time? And what about the attentions of that personable man in the office? Should she rebuff him because they hadn't had the preliminary of a formal introduction?

Something had to give, and what gave, eventually, was the notion of a chaperon. "The youth of to-day," concedes an author in 1923, "has relegated the chaperone to the lumber room along with mid-victorian furniture and relics of another age." As etiquette books gathered dust on working women's shelves, the authors sensed their growing unpopularity. They weren't keeping up with the times, a colleague criticized in 1935, for there was barely an etiquette book "that the present-day working girl could use as a guide in her social contact with the opposite sex, and be anything but a hermit."

At the job interview a job seeker should:

"Stand until you are invited to sit; do not make a dive for the nearest chair, and drag it squealingly up to the desk, close to the man you have come to see. Many a man, and woman, have lost out permanently with such an awkward beginning."

ETIQUETTE UP-TO-DATE
Mrs. Cornelius Beeckman, 1938

"[T]he business woman . . . must above all things avoid the pretty little airs and graces, the charming ways which are so delightful in a parlor, but which are utterly out of place, nay, even dangerous, in the arena of daily struggle for bread and butter."

SOCIAL CUSTOMS
Florence Howe Hall, 1911

"Weeping just doesn't belong in business."

MANNERS IN BUSINESS
Elizabeth Gregg MacGibbon, 1954

"[T]he business woman . . . must above all things avoid the pretty
little airs and graces, the charming ways which are so delightful in
a parlor, but which are utterly out of place, nay, even dangerous,
in the arena of daily struggle for bread and butter."

"Artists, alone, may gratify their taste for velvet jackets, Tam-o'-Shanters, and Windsor ties, but the privilege is denied business men. Eccentricity of dress usually indicates eccentricity of temper, and we do not want temperamental business men. It is hard enough to get along with authors and artists and musicians."

THE BOOK OF BUSINESS ETIQUETTE
Anonymous, 1922

"Diamonds should not be worn during business hours by men who are obliged to stand behind counters or engage in any toil."

SOCIAL ETIQUETTE
Maud C. Cooke, 18—

"Occasionally the dread of dreads happens. When space is a problem at conventions or at large away-from home sales meetings, participants are sometimes required to share a room. Most men would rather have all of their fingernails slowly removed. . . .

"All business hotels have twin beds now, so there's no problem there. If the beds are together to form a double bed, separate them of course. Don't, however, go pushing the bed clear across the room, casting suspicious and indignant glances all the while at your roomy."

ESQUIRE'S GUIDE TO MODERN ETIQUETTE
The Editors of Esquire *magazine and Ron Butler, 1969*

"Needless to say, don't ever ask for an autograph in a men's room, even though the situation does seem to put you on an equal footing."

ESQUIRE'S GUIDE TO MODERN ETIQUETTE
The Editors of Esquire *magazine and Ron Butler, 1969*

•　　　•　　　•

"To ask a really important person to sign an autograph book full of the names of nobodies is to insult him, no matter how graciously he may rise to the occasion in his acceptance of the request—or more probably, in his refusal."

AMY VANDERBILT'S ETIQUETTE
Amy Vanderbilt, 1972

"Elevator operators, except for normal pleasantries, should be firmly discouraged from venturing into conversations with passengers. They should also not be allowed to perform, sing, whistle or dance, as many are inclined to do at the expense of captured audiences."

ESQUIRE'S GUIDE TO MODERN ETIQUETTE
The Editors of Esquire *magazine and Ron Butler, 1969*

"Most people object to the physical nearness of others. It is the thing that makes the New York subways during the rush hours such a horror. . . . A safe rule is never to touch another person. He may resent it."

THE BOOK OF BUSINESS ETIQUETTE
Anonymous, 1922

"It is a sign of ill-breeding to change your seat in a car or omnibus. If you are unfortunate enough to have a neighbor who is positively annoying and unendurable, it is better to get out and take the next conveyance than to move to the other side."

FROST'S LAWS AND BY-LAWS OF AMERICAN SOCIETY
S. A. Frost, 1869

"It is the correct thing to ask a person sitting in the same seat with yourself if he would like to look at your newspaper."

THE CORRECT THING IN GOOD SOCIETY
Florence Howe Hall, 1902

•   •   •

"It's a great idea to file your finger nails in the street car, bus, or train. It's certainly making the most of your time. The noise of the filing drowns the unpleasant noise of the wheels. But it is the act of an ill-bred person. Who but an ordinary would allow her epithelium to fly all over? I should think that one might as well scatter ashes after a cremation, around the neighborhood."

MANNERS FOR MILLIONS
Sophie C. Hadida, 1932

ON THE TOWN

It was not enough for a male pedestrian to don his hat and walking stick in order to saunter down the street. He had to be up on his manly arts, particularly boxing. "The power to deliver a good scientific blow may be of inestimable value under certain extreme circumstances . . ." instructs an author, for a man "may come upon some ruffian insulting a woman in the streets; and in such cases a blow settles the matter." The discreet gentleman did not accompany his punches with a narration of wrath, for there was a way to fight gracefully and that is in silence. "Never assail an offender with words, nor when you strike him, use such expressions as, 'Take that,' &c," counsels a male writer. While it is not "precisely good manners" to send a fellow pedestrian reeling curbside, he concedes, "to omit it is sometimes very bad manners. . . ." Therefore, to know how to box and how to box well was "an important accomplishment, particularly for little men."

"[F]or a young lady to be seen walking alone is most undesirable. If she cannot walk with her younger sisters and their governess, or the maid cannot be spared to walk with her, she had better stay at home or confine herself to the square garden."

THE MANNERS OF THE ARISTOCRACY
By One of Themselves, 18—

"*Never assail an offender with words, nor when you strike him, use such expressions as, 'Take that,' &c.*"

"Walk on the street-side of the sidewalk when you can do it gracefully. There are few run-away horses, these days, but there are still splashing puddles and other terrors of the street from which you can 'protect' your woman companion. It is better, however, to walk on the inside than to convert a simple stroll into a ballet: don't cross back and forth behind her or be forever running around end just to get into position. The rule is supposed to be for her comfort and her safety; she finds nothing comfortable about talking to a whirling dervish."

ESQUIRE ETIQUETTE
The Editors of Esquire *magazine, 1953*

"A gentleman must never take a lady's arm or take hold of her by or above the elbow and push her hither or thither."

THE BOOK OF GOOD MANNERS
Victor H. Diescher, 1923

"If a lady and gentleman are walking arm in arm, they should keep step. The gentleman must adapt his long stride to her shorter steps, else they have a curious appearance."

POLITE SOCIETY AT HOME AND ABROAD
Mrs. Annie R. White, 1891

"If a gentleman is walking with two ladies in a rain storm, and there is but one umbrella, he should give it to his companions and walk outside. Nothing can be more absurd than to see a gentleman walking between two ladies holding an umbrella which perfectly protects himself, but half deluges his companions with its dripping streams."

OUR DEPORTMENT
Compiled by John H. Young, 1881

• • •

"In carrying an umbrella or a cane under your arm, do not publish your awkwardness by carrying it in such a way as to make a cross of yourself, with the lance end sticking out behind you, endangering the eyes of others."

THE MENTOR
Alfred Ayres, 1894

"Do not carry your umbrella in your arms like a baby . . ."

MANNERS FOR GIRLS
Mrs. Humphry, 1901

"In case of a sudden fall of rain, you may, with perfect propriety, offer your umbrella to a lady who is unprovided with one. If she accepts it, and asks your address to return it, leave it with her; if she hesitates, and does not wish to deprive you of the use of it, you may offer to accompany her to her destination, and then, do not open a conversation; let your manner be respectful, and when you leave her, let her thank you, assure her of the pleasure it has given you to be of service, bow, and leave her."

THE GENTLEMEN'S BOOK OF ETIQUETTE AND MANUAL OF POLITENESS
Cecil B. Hartley, 1860

"A young man once asked me if it would be etiquette to offer an unknown lady an umbrella in the street, supposing she stood in need of one. I replied: 'No *lady* would accept the offer from a stranger, and the other sort of person might never return the umbrella.' "

MANNERS FOR MEN
Mrs. Humphry, 1897

"No lady will be guilty of the vulgarity of sucking the head of her parasol in the street."

FROST'S LAWS AND BY-LAWS OF AMERICAN SOCIETY
S. A. Frost, 1869

"What are you doing? Sucking the head of your parasol! Have you not break-fasted? Take that piece of ivory from your mouth! To suck it is unlady-like, and let me tell you, excessively unbecoming."

THE LADIES' BOOK OF ETIQUETTE, AND MANUAL OF POLITENESS
Florence Hartley, 1873

"It is offending against good taste as well as against common sense, however, to walk through the streets in the wintry season clad in slippers so thin and stockings so transparent that they make the beholder shiver."

GOOD FORM FOR ALL OCCASIONS
Florence Howe Hall, 1914

"If stormy weather has made it necessary to lay a plank across the gutters, which has become suddenly filled with water, it is not proper to crowd before another, in order to pass over the frail bridge."

MANNERS, CULTURE AND DRESS OF THE BEST AMERICAN SOCIETY
Richard A. Wells, 1890

"When you see persons slip down on the ice, do not laugh at them."

MISS LESLIE'S BEHAVIOUR BOOK
Miss Leslie, 1859

"No gentleman is guilty of smoking when walking or riding with a lady. It leaves the impression with others that she is of secondary importance to his cigar."

POLITE SOCIETY AT HOME AND ABROAD
Mrs. Annie R. White, 1891

"Smoking in the streets, or in a theatre, is only practised by shop-boys, pseudo-fashionables—and the 'SWELL MOB.' "

HINTS ON ETIQUETTE
Charles William Day, 1843

*"Talking to one's self is a bad habit because one is
likely to indulge in it when walking on the street."*

"Frenchmen of all classes regard it as quite proper to ask a passer by in the street or on the hotel terrace, for a light for a cigar or cigarette. When the American is requested to lend fire from his fragrant weed, he must do so unhesitatingly. The cigar or cigarette must be held out so that the would be smoker can touch its tip with his own, and a match should in no case be offered in place of the lighted cigar. To do so would be to slightly insult the petitioner for the favour and when the light has been secured, and the stranger lifts his hat with murmured thanks, it is necessary for the perhaps astonished American to lift his own and assume the expression of one who grudges not in the least to oblige a fellow smoker."

ENCYCLOPAEDIA OF ETIQUETTE
Emily Holt, 1901

"There are good physiological reasons why the incessant chewing of anything is injurious, and it certainly is not in good taste to see persons in school or other public places with their mouths full of gum or wax, and apparently in laborious exercise. Such rumination is very unbecoming on the street, and, if observed, would give rise to serious doubts whether the ruminant be a lady or not."

GOOD MORALS AND GENTLE MANNERS
Alex M. Gow, 1873

"Never pull the gum out in long strings."

MANNERS FOR MILLIONS
Sophie C. Hadida, 1932

•　　•　　•

"Dessert is the only course that may be properly eaten while strolling on the sidewalk, and only certain desserts, at that. Apples, bananas, and pears are acceptable; peaches and grapefruit are not. Ice cream cones and chocolate bars are fine, but pineapple upsidedown cake is out. You will notice that dessert means that no meats or vegetables are permitted, nor are the usual breakfast foods, such as pancakes with maple syrup or eggs once over lightly."

MISS MANNER'S GUIDE TO EXCRUCIATINGLY CORRECT BEHAVIOR
Judith Martin, 1982

"There are some ill-mannered and malicious persons, who take pleasure in misleading strangers by wrong directions. It will be enough to mention such impertinence in order to despise it as we ought."

THE GENTLEMAN AND LADY'S BOOK OF POLITENESS
Mme. Celnart, 1835

"Do not cross abruptly in front of another person, nor stop dead in your tracks, causing the man behind to bump into you."

THE BOOK OF GOOD MANNERS
Victor H. Diescher, 1923

"To look back at one who has passed, even if she has on a new dress which does not fit in the back, is not polite."

THE MANNERS THAT WIN
Anonymous, 1880

"Stopping to stare in the shop-windows is against the rules of strict etiquette."

FROST'S LAWS AND BY-LAWS OF AMERICAN SOCIETY
S. A. Frost, 1869

•　　•　　•

"Do not stop to join a crowd who are collected round a street show, or street merchant, unless you wish to pass for a countryman taking a holiday in the city."

THE GENTLEMEN'S BOOK OF ETIQUETTE AND MANUAL OF POLITENESS
Cecil B. Hartley, 1860

"Girls, never, never turn at a whistle, to see if you are wanted. A whistle is usually to call a dog."

GOOD MANNERS
Beth Bailey McLean, 1934

"Talking to one's self is a bad habit because one is likely to indulge in it when walking on the street."

MANNERS FOR MILLIONS
Sophie C. Hadida, 1932

"Of the unspeakable savages who make night hideous sometimes by shouting and singing in quiet streets in the small hours of the morning my pen refuses to write."

GOOD MANNERS AND BAD
Hugh Scott, 1930

CHANCE MEETINGS

"Should you, while walking with your friend, meet an acquaintance, never introduce them," advises a count in his etiquette book. "There are many reasons why people ought never to be introduced to the acquaintance of each other, without the consent of each party previously obtained," he elaborates. "[A] stupid person may be delighted with the society of a man of learning or talent, to whom in return such an acquaintance may prove an annoyance and a clog, as one incapable of offering an interchange of thought, or an idea worth listening to."

"Be very guarded about introducing titled foreigners to young ladies. Sometimes titles are not open to inspection."

Etiquette experts had advice for the baroness stuck with the unseemly new acquaintance. "The best way to be rid of an embarrassing acquaintance-ship is to strangle it in its birth," recommends one author. Cultivate "an unsee-ing, preoccupied glance that does not rest upon its object. . . ." If, on the street, the common-born "Mrs. Brown or Mrs. Jones persist in bowing, re-turn the bow, but return it with studied coldness," adds another.

Snobbery had its perils, however, as illustrated by this story recounted in several etiquette books: "Most people have heard of the gentleman (?) who was perfect in his knowledge of the laws of etiquette, and who, seeing a man drowning, took off his coat and was about to plunge into the water to rescue him, when he suddenly remembered that he had never been introduced to the struggling victim, and resuming his coat, tranquilly proceeded upon his way. . . . Too rigid an observance of the laws of etiquette makes them an ab-surdity and a nuisance."

"To bow or not to bow is often a puzzling question."

THE BOOK OF ETIQUETTE
Lady Troubridge, 1931

"When a lady appears on the street with a veil over her face, it may sometimes be a sign that she does not wish to be recognized, and an acquaintance may pass her as a stranger, without either giving or taking offense."

GOOD MORALS AND GENTLE MANNERS
Alex M. Gow, 1873

"[N]o man may stop to speak to a lady until she stops to speak to him. The lady, in short, has the right in all cases to be friendly or distant. Women have not many rights; let us gracefully concede the few that they possess."

THE HABITS OF GOOD SOCIETY
Anonymous, 1859

•   •   •

"A gentleman will raise his hat fairly from the head, and not limit his salutation to a mere touch of the rim, like a coachman or a waiter."

THE BAZAR BOOK OF DECORUM
Anonymous, 1870

"A young woman should remember that when a woman's salutation ceases to be delicate, elegant and finished, that she steps down from her throne and throws away her sceptre."

THE AMERICAN CODE OF MANNERS
Anonymous, 1880

"When a lady, who has been introduced to a gentleman, so far forgets good taste and good manners, as to make herself conspicuous by rouged cheeks, enamelled complexion, blackened eyelids, or vulgarities of dress or conduct, no gentleman can be blamed for avoiding her eyes, and if she is so far lost to a sense of womanly behavior as still to seek recognition, the cut direct would scarcely wound her feelings."

THE MANNERS THAT WIN
Anonymous, 1880

"The right hand of a gentleman is the place occupied by his wife and ladies of her class, either in walking or driving; any woman seen on his left hand may be taken for someone outside of social recognition."

STANDARD ETIQUETTE FOR ALL OCCASIONS
Ethel Cushing Brant, 1925

"It is not polite to stare under ladies' bonnets, as if you suspected they had stolen the linings from you, or wore something that was not their own."

THE LADIES' BOOK OF ETIQUETTE, AND MANUAL OF POLITENESS
Florence Hartley, 1873

•   •   •

"If you meet or join or are visited by a person who has any article whatever, under his arm or in his hand, and he does not offer to show it to you, you should not, even if it be your most intimate friend, take it from him and look at it."

OUR DEPORTMENT
Compiled by John H. Young, 1881

"Don't let some one go through the process of introducing a boy to you, and then say merrily, 'Ha-ha! I've known him for years.' That's hateful."

PERSONALITY PREFERRED!
Elizabeth Woodward, 1935

"Be very guarded about introducing titled foreigners to young ladies. Sometimes titles are not open to inspection."

TWENTIETH CENTURY ETIQUETTE
Annie Randall White, 1900

Chapter 9

MANNERS FOR TOURISTS AND TRAVELERS

And Other Sightseers

SUNDAY DRIVERS

By the early 1900s a speedy new pastime had captured the populace: Motoring. "The rage for automobiling has swept over our land, like a wave of temporary insanity," observes an author in 1911. "And with its growing favor has sprung up a noxious and flourishing crop of bad manners," complains a colleague.

Soon etiquette authors were devoting sections of their books to this new sport. "The wealthy and generous owner of a large touring automobile who invites a party of friends to fill the seats of his fine vehicle and spend with him a week doing the chateaux on the Loire, or the cathedrals of southern England, or the picturesque roads of Massachusetts, must be prepared to bear all the expenses incurred," instructs an author. He must never gleefully zip past dramatic gorges or waterfalls, impatiently refusing to stop at points of interest, nor exasperate his party by motoring at the pace of a snail, fearful of the machinery at his disposal. He must stop regularly for roadside luncheons and teas, ever ready with a hamper full of hot and cold refreshments. And he must offer to his passengers, at the outset, blankets, dust-cloaks, and goggles for the dusty tour ahead.

The motorcar guest, in turn, must learn to cultivate an air of enjoyment for the greatest of inconveniences, for it was an unpardonable faux pas "[t]o sulk or sit in moody silence," scolds a writer. Even if the Model T spun off the road and ended in a crunch against a tree, the diplomatic passenger must be "able to meet an accident and long roadside wait with a buoyant air of enjoying an amusing experience . . ." she orders.

"Ladies do not usually motor alone with gentlemen unless they are engaged or are relatives."

ETIQUETTE FOR LADIES
Anonymous, 1925

"It may be added that any attempt to keep up in motoring fashions will result in insanity or inebriety."

A BACHELOR'S CUPBOARD
A. Lyman Phillips, 1906

"Those who remember the earlier days of motoring will recall the invariably unattractive appearance of the woman who motored—a shapeless bundle in cumbersome cloak and hood, heavily veiled and wearing clumsy goggles, looking in fact a perfect fright!—but common sense, improved cars and modern dress artists have changed all that, and Eve in the car, whether she be driver or passenger, is daintily chic, smart, and attractive."

ETIQUETTE UP TO DATE
Constance Burleigh, 1925

"When you are stopped at a red signal, don't gun your motor to make old ladies jump when they cross in front of your car."

MCCALL'S BOOK OF EVERYDAY ETIQUETTE
Margaret Bevans with the Editors of McCall's *magazine, 1960*

•　　•　　•

"And don't exhibit to all the cars behind you your childish affection for stuffed teddy bears, tigers, or dogs with wagging heads, for all of them are simply signs announcing in all languages: 'The owner of this car has vulgar taste.' "

ACCENT ON ELEGANCE
Geneviève Antoine Dariaux, 1970

"Drive with special care if you have a clergy or Jesus Saves sign on the rear of your car."

CHRISTIAN ETIQUETTE
Lora Lee Parrott, 1953

"Don't fail to have your tires cleaned after using them, as this attention will prolong their life."

DON'TS FOR EVERYBODY
Compiled by Frederic Reddale, 1907

"Don't try to lift her, throw her in, or do any other 'cute' little thing of that sort. Girls think about damage to shoes and clothes, and generally each has her own way of getting in and out of a rumble."

MANNERS FOR MODERNS
Kathleen Black, 1938

"It's unsafe to engage in passionate efforts while driving a car. If, in the car, are another couple who are not too well acquainted, it's unfair to force them to watch your amorous struggle while they carry on a faltering conversation about 'My favorite composers are . . .' "

ETIQUETTE ETC.
Shelia Ostrander, 1967

"Above all, be wary of the female hitch hiker. She may be a sweet girl, but she may also be an expert blackmailer."

THE CORRECT THING
William Oliver Stevens, 1934

PULLMAN PROPRIETY

"One of the easiest ways to distinguish real folks from poor white trash is to observe them on trains . . ." reveals an etiquette writer. The sight of a famished Pullman passenger struggling with a slithery sandwich offered an excellent opportunity to scrutinize pedigree. "The best and most convenient of all out-of-door edibles, is the sandwich," recommends an author— that is, the sandwich made of ground meat and "[n]ot the one with slips of meat laid between slices of buttered bread, so that when a bite of bread is taken, all the enclosed meat is dragged out, unless a serious contest takes place in its behalf between the teeth and fingers, which, to confess the truth, is not an attractive conflict, as every one will attest who ever saw a party of railway-travellers, each at war with one of them, as the train moved out from a way-station where the conductor had cried out 'five minutes for refreshments!' "

The disposal of luncheon remains was another gauge of breeding. A punctilious passenger did not deposit his rinds in the aisle for female passengers to sweep up with the hems of their skirts. "Spit in a spitoon, and throw refuse out the window," insists an etiquette expert. Which window to raise was a tricky decision, for opening the wrong one transgressed into the realm of rudeness. "At any time it is decidedly inconsiderate and a breach of courtesy to open a window on that side of the coach from which the smoke and cinders, flying from the engine, cannot fail to pour in upon the other occupants of the car," explains a writer.

Pullman pollution was so common an occurrence that many etiquette authors offered remedies for its effects. "A horse hair twisted into a loop carefully inserted under the eyelid will remove cinders," tips one book. If a horse hair was not available, get out at the next station and procure a bristle-hair from a sweeping-brush, tips a second.

Trapped in a jiggling seat, eyes full of cinders and stomach full of mashed meat, the rider of rails may not have felt the steadiest. Not to worry, the writers report, there are solutions even for that: "Here is a remedy for nausea, or sickness of the stomach, with which so many persons are afflicted while on a

"Pajamas are good for sleeping car and in case of a wreck or collision a man may under the circumstances be considered properly dressed."

railway journey: Take a sheet of heavy writing paper large enough to cover both chest and stomach, pasting two or three together if necessary, as stomach and chest must be well covered. Wear this continuously, changing it daily if the journey is a long one. Although very simple, this remedy is effective and well worth trying."

"Don't trail up and down a Pullman in a floating, peach-colored negligee, frothy with lace or feathers. It might put you over in a big way in a boudoir, but not on a train."

COMPETE!
Frances Angell, 1935

"Pajamas are good for sleeping car and in case of a wreck or collision a man may under the circumstances be considered properly dressed."

SOCIAL CONDUCT
The Church of Jesus Christ of Latter-day Saints, 1934

"Forgetting the number of one's berth and blundering into the wrong place is a serious breach of good manners in a sleeping car, and it is extremely severe on timid persons who have gone to bed with visions before their minds of the man who was murdered in lower ten and the woman who brought her husband's corpse from Florida in the same berth with her."

THE BOOK OF BUSINESS ETIQUETTE
Anonymous, 1922

"Ladies traveling alone should consult conductors or captains. Ladies will thank gentlemen who raise or lower windows, coldly but politely."

COLLIER'S CYCLOPEDIA OF COMMERCIAL AND SOCIAL INFORMATION
Compiled by Nugent Robinson, 1882

"It is especially the duty of ladies to look after other ladies younger or less experienced than themselves who may be traveling without escort. To watch these and see that they are not made the dupes of villains, and to pass a pleasant word with others who may possibly feel the loneliness of their situation, should be the especial charge of every lady of experience."

SOCIAL CULTURE
Anonymous, 1903

"[U]nless you are previously certain of her respectability, have little to say to a woman who is travelling without a companion, and whose face is painted, who wears a profusion of long curls about her neck, who has a meretricious expression of eye, and who is over-dressed. It is safest to avoid her."

MISS LESLIE'S BEHAVIOUR BOOK
Miss Leslie, 1859

"Don't use the word 'ride' when you should say 'drive.' You don't 'ride' in a carriage, a 'bus, or a train—you drive."

ETIQUETTE FOR WOMEN
G. R. M. Devereux, 1902

DECK DECORUM

There were often as many sharks on the decks of an ocean liner as in the waters below. "Do not rashly make acquaintances on board, and never enter freely into business conversations with strangers, nor join them in any game of hazard, unless you are very quick at spotting fraud and trickery," warns an etiquette writer. "Because of the numbers of people of wealth who travel to Europe," another explains, "many crooks desirous of acquiring easy money take the trip and endeavor to ingratiate themselves with such people; therefore it is well not to play cards for money with strangers, as many a poor victim who has foolishly done so, will testify." But cardsharps were not the only villains. Even an innocent-seeming deck-chair neighbor may have ulterior motives. "It is the correct thing to remember that the reporter also travelleth, and to be wary of what one says to strangers," cautions one writer. Don't relax even back in your cabin: "[R]emember that the partition-walls on steamers and ships and even in hotels, are very thin, and to avoid reciting one's family history loud enough for the occupant of the next stateroom or chamber to hear it." But then again, don't ruin your trip by letting your caution become paranoia: "Only a prig refuses to speak to a man on a train or a boat because he does not know his name," concludes a colleague.

"It is not usual for a woman to travel across the ocean alone."

BOOK OF ETIQUETTE, vol. II
Lillian Eichler, 1921

"Avoid failing to notice Etna, Vesuvius, Fujiyama, flying fish, icebergs, or other objects of interest, because you are immersed in tea, deck quoits, sleep, drinks at the bar, or a novel, or the ship's pool, whether the betting or swimming variety."

CAN I HELP YOU?
Viola Tree, 1937

"Why cannot a man wear a fairly decent garment when bathing, instead of the sleeveless, almost backless, garment that is now so generally affected? If a man cannot swim with a sleeve that covers his shoulder, he should give up bathing in company that includes women."

THE BOOK OF GOOD MANNERS
Mrs. Burton Kingsland, 1901

"It is hardly necessary for us to say that no modest, well-bred woman, will wear the close fitting and abbreviated costumes sometimes seen, alas! with too evident an intent to display one's charms. The legs and sleeves should be long, the neck high, and the costume loose and full."

MODERN MANNERS AND SOCIAL FORMS
Julia M. Bradley, 1889

"If you are sick yourself, say as little about it as possible. . . . At no time talk about it to gentlemen. . . ."

"It is not the correct thing to say, in case of a slight squall at sea, 'Captain, is there *any hope left?*' "

THE CORRECT THING IN GOOD SOCIETY
Florence Howe Hall, 1902

"If you are sick yourself, say as little about it as possible. . . . At no time talk about it to gentlemen. Many foolish commonplace sayings are uttered by ladies who attempt to describe the horrors of sea-sickness. For instance this—'I felt all the time as if I wished somebody to take me up, and throw me overboard.' This is untrue—no human being ever really *did* prefer drowning to sea-sickness."

MISS LESLIE'S BEHAVIOUR BOOK
Miss Leslie, 1859

"Spike heels are no good for rolling days at sea."

THE ARMY WIFE
Nancy Shea; revised by Anna Perle Smith, 1966

"[D]o not try to show your courage by indulging in undue gayety. Mirth is out of place when the sky is overcast with gloom, the wind blowing hard, and the waves 'running mountains high,' and foaming and roaring all round the vessel."

MISS LESLIE'S BEHAVIOUR BOOK
Miss Leslie, 1859

"No lady should stand or linger in the halls of a hotel, but pass through them quietly, never stopping alone for a moment."

THE LADY LODGER

There was something unseemly about a lone woman staying in public lodgings, and hotel decorum reflected this. A lady must never be seen entering or exiting through the main doors of a hotel: "There is always an entrance for ladies especially, and it is bold and unbecoming for them to be seen in the one appropriated to gentlemen," warns a writer. She must never appear to dawdle: "No lady should stand or linger in the halls of a hotel, but pass through them quietly, never stopping alone for a moment." She must avoid all displays of her occupancy: "No lady should stand alone at the front windows of a hotel parlor, nor may she walk out on the porch, or, indeed, any conspicuous place." It was not enough for her character to be immaculate, explains a writer: "To avoid the appearance of evil, as well as the evil itself, is important in the case of every woman." Such precautions were essential: "Ladies," confides a woman, "know how the shadow of suspicion withers and torments them."

"For a lady to go up the stairs of a hotel humming a tune is ill-bred, and may expose her to rudeness."

GOOD MANNERS FOR ALL OCCASIONS
Margaret E. Sangster, 1921

"No lady should use the piano of a hotel uninvited if there are others in the room. It looks bold and forward to display even the most finished musical education in this way. It is still worse to sing."

FROST'S LAWS AND BY-LAWS OF AMERICAN SOCIETY
S. A. Frost, 1869

"[S]ome punishment should be devised for a young girl who cannot play, yet has the folly and assurance to seat herself at the piano of a public parlour, and annoy the company by an hour of tinking and tanking with one finger only."

MISS LESLIE'S BEHAVIOUR BOOK
Miss Leslie, 1859

"It is a breach of etiquette for a lady to touch her baggage in a hotel after it is packed. There are plenty of servants to attend to it, and they should carry to the hack even the travelling-shawl, satchel, and railway novel. Nothing looks more awkward than to see a lady, with both hands full, stumbling up the steps of a hotel hack."

FROST'S LAWS AND BY-LAWS OF AMERICAN SOCIETY
S. A. Frost, 1869

Chapter 10

MANNERS
FOR TOMBOYS
AND SISSIES
And Other Children

HOME SWEET HOME

"[H]omes are often deadly dull, insipid to weariness. They are deserts of monotony," confides one writer. "In some houses, the father dozes on the lounge all the evening. The boys skip out of the house the moment supper is over. You see no more of them till a late bedtime. By and by they form undesirable associations—get into bad company, start on the downhill road. It is not too much to say that fun at home would have saved many a lad from ruin."

Use games to keep your children on the straight and narrow, suggest the etiquette writers. After dessert, dangle sugar lumps off the ends of fishing rods and try to catch them with your mouth. Play a game of "Boiled Egg": Simply place one hard-boiled egg among an uncooked dozen and then try to single it out ("spin them around; those unboiled or semi-liquid inside, will spin with a waddling motion, while the hard egg will spin like a top"). Or conduct a "Fire-light Party": Gather the family in front of the hearth and provide each player with a bundle of twigs. Don't forget to turn down the gas lamps first, as there should be "no light except that furnished by the open fire," instructs one etiquette book. Going in succession, each family member tosses his or her bundle into the flames and while it burns, that person "is expected to sing a song, tell a story, give a recitation, or otherwise amuse the company."

Alas, by 1922 no amount of parlor tricks or charades could keep the youth at home. The excitements of modern life had surpassed the quiet charm of family togetherness. "The days are gone when the family sat in the evening around the fire, or a 'table with a lamp,' when it was customary to read aloud or to talk. Few people 'talk well' in these days; fewer read aloud, and fewer still endure listening to any book literally word by word," sighs Emily Post. "To the over-busy or gaily fashionable, 'home' might as well be a railroad station, and members of a family passengers who see each other only for a few hurried minutes before taking trains in opposite directions."

"To be polite to everybody except the people they love most is a nervous affectation that afflicts many families otherwise normal. They struggle into their manners as they might squeeze themselves into Grandma's wedding dress, and when they come home, they take off their smiles and soft words, and sit about, spiritually in their underwear. This isn't pretty."

SAFE CONDUCT
Margaret Fishback, 1938

"To set the table with a spotted cloth, to stand the milk bottle on the cloth, adding rings to spots, to put a dirtied bib around a child's neck, to permit a man to sit at table in his undershirt or a woman with her hair in curlers, is to create a destroying influence against which good manners collapse."

CHILDREN ARE PEOPLE
Emily Post, 1940

"When mother or father enters the living room, the children should immediately rise to their feet and wait until they have selected their chairs."

CULTURE AND GOOD MANNERS
Ethel Frey Cushing, 1926

"It is not too much to say that fun at home
would have saved many a lad from ruin."

"The man who stands with his hat on in the presence of his mother and sister, manifests thereby such a want of apprehension of the requirements of filial and fraternal reverence and affection—of the rudiments of true domestic loyalty—as, if circumstances do not combine to correct him, will in the long-run render him fit for treason, stratagems, and spoils; he sets at naught feelings and principles which would interpose one of the most important barriers between himself and crime. It would not be surprising if such a man were to finish his career in the dock or the hulks; he lacks the true nobility and elevation of sentiment without which he will not, and he cannot, come to good."

THE STANDARD BOOK ON POLITENESS, GOOD BEHAVIOR AND
SOCIAL ETIQUETTE
Anonymous, 1884

"It is not the correct thing for parents to obey their children."

THE CORRECT THING IN GOOD SOCIETY
Florence Howe Hall, 1902

"It is not the correct thing to take offence if a neighbor states civilly that he would prefer your children should cease from breaking his windows."

THE CORRECT THING IN GOOD SOCIETY
Florence Howe Hall, 1902

"Many boys seize things which are shown them in a rough manner, and pull them to pieces. Their fond parents excuse this destructive tendency as the act of an 'inquiring mind,' that 'must know the ins and outs of everything,' but we would prefer a boy to be a little less inquisitive, and a little more of a gentleman."

THE NEW CENTURY PERFECT SPEAKER
Edited by John Coulter, 1901

"Peevish temper, cross and frowning faces, and uncomely looks have sometimes been cured in France by sending the child into an octagonal boudoir lined

"Do not leave children to their own devices near a lion's cage."

with looking-glasses, where, whichever way it turned, it would see the reflection of its own unpleasant features, and be constrained, out of self-respect, to assume a more amiable disposition."

GOOD BEHAVIOR
Anonymous, 1876

"A little frivolity is to be expected in the young; a thoroughly staid, severe, and solemn young person is an anachronism."

GOOD MANNERS FOR ALL OCCASIONS
Margaret E. Sangster, 1921

"Neither a child nor any one else should be permitted to be in the glare of the sun without his hat. If he be allowed, he is likely to have a sun-stroke, which might either at once kill him, or might make him an idiot for the remainder of his life, which latter would be the worse alternative of the two."

WOMAN AS A WIFE AND MOTHER
Pye Henry Chavasse, 1870

"Do not leave children to their own devices near a lion's cage."

GOOD MANNERS FOR ALL OCCASIONS
Margaret E. Sangster, 1921

"Do not give food such as bread, toast, cookies, pickles, crackers, fruit, shelled nuts, candies to your child from your hands. He is a human; not a squirrel."

MANNERS FOR MILLIONS
Sophie C. Hadida, 1932

Chapter 11

MANNERS
FOR CORPSES
AND WIDOWS
And Other Mourners

DEATHBED DECORUM

One's manner, when dead, was just as important as when alive. "The human body, even in the unconsciousness of death, continues to be the object of a punctilious observance of ceremony," explains a writer. So licensed, etiquette authors offered advice for the corpse with the same exuberance as for the living.

If the deceased was betrothed, snatched from her fiancé's arms, she should wear in her coffin what she wished to wear down the aisle, one author instructs. But if she was a little girl, too young for the fires of courtship, "virginal robes of spotless white should invest her, symbolic of her stainless grace and purity." "For women a night-dress or wrapper aids the illusion that they have fallen asleep," tips another.

Some found the directives of etiquette an intrusion at this time. "It is cruel to enhance sorrow by binding it around with the silken serpent of etiquette," one writer protests. But others gained comfort in the constraints of orders and rules to follow. A colleague retorts: "Courtesy is the guardian angel of the survivors when a home is touched by the finger of the Grim Reaper."

Perhaps the dying should have the final word. It is said that Lord Chesterfield, famed for his letters on conduct, was as concerned with manners in his final moments as he had been during his lifetime. His last utterance was (Day-rolles was a visitor): "Give Dayrolles a chair."

"Should your friend look ill, do not tell her so. People have been gently pushed into their graves by overzealous friends who have noticed how ill they look."

GOOD MANNERS FOR ALL OCCASIONS
Margaret E. Sangster, 1921

"Never talk in a perfunctory manner when you call at a house of mourning."

GOOD MANNERS FOR ALL OCCASIONS
Margaret E. Sangster, 1921

"It is impossible to attempt to be polite without cultivating a good memory. The absent or self-absorbed person who . . . speaks of the dead as if they were living . . . will never succeed in society."

MANNERS AND SOCIAL USAGES
Mrs. John Sherwood, 1897

"Avoid inquiring the state of mind of a departed friend, or relative, when paying a visit of condolence. This may cause mental distress to the survivors; for the deceased may have led an irregular life, and his death-bed may not have been so happy as could have been wished."

THE LADY'S BOOK OF MANNERS
Anonymous, 1870

"In calling on friends who have suffered bereavement, after having received their card of thanks for kind inquiries, it is, of course, requisite that the dress should be of the quietest description. A red tie, for instance, would be horribly out of place."

MANNERS FOR MEN
Mrs. Humphry, 1897

"Courtesy is the guardian angel of the survivors when a home is touched by the finger of the Grim Reaper."

"Some one has said that the custom of allowing the curious who did not know the deceased, and who cared nothing for him, to gaze on his face after death, seems to be taking an unfair advantage of the dead."

EVERYDAY ETIQUETTE
Marion Harland and Virginia Van de Water, 1907

"Another absurd and unhealthy habit of kissing with women, which is even worse and more stupid than the cat and dog business, is the kissing of dead folks. What possible pleasure can there be to a living person to perform such an act? and as far as the dead are concerned, they might as well kiss a bed-post; and as far as their own health is concerned, it would be much better for them to do so. I heard of one woman who got the small-pox by kissing a man who died with it. She was probably more anxious to kiss him after he was dead than when he was living."

HUMAN NATURE
Prof. A. E. Willis, 1907

ASHES TO ASHES

"At funerals—talk to no one," one author commands. "If you should by chance catch the eye of some one who bows to you—just look away." If it was imperative to communicate, do so inaudibly: "If you cannot deliver a necessary message at any other time, then silently put a note written on anything into the hand of the one to whom you must speak."

Expressions of emotion were as taboo as conversation, and conditions leading to them were to be avoided whenever possible. If women were to be present when the casket was lowered into the ground, the grave should be lined with leafy branches to lessen the impression of bare soil. And cold, damp, dark "[e]arth is never placed on the coffin until the family and friends depart," insists an authority.

Flowers thrown onto the lowering coffin do not absolve the living from debts of love or attention: "Flowers on the coffin cast no fragrance backward over the weary days," chides a writer. Nor do elaborate tombstones compensate for misspent lives: "[E]tiquette unites with the laws of beauty and refined sentiment in protesting against the erecting of hideous monuments with absurd inscriptions," argues an author. "The purpose of the tombstone is to mark the resting place and to bear the name and the date of the birth and death of the person who lies beneath it. If the life itself has not left a record that will last a marble slab will not do much to perpetuate it."

"Do not slight an invitation to a funeral."

POLITE SOCIETY AT HOME AND ABROAD
Mrs. Annie R. White, 1891

"Finally, let it be said, and emphatically, that none but the prying vulgarian will attempt to attend the funeral of a total stranger, unless the deceased is a person of such reputation that his or her obsequies assume a public or semi-public character."

ENCYCLOPAEDIA OF ETIQUETTE
Emily Holt, 1901

"No longer is it permissible to follow the curious old-fashioned custom of sending an empty carriage to drive in a funeral procession in token of the respect which the owner was prevented from showing by appearing in person."

ENCYCLOPAEDIA OF ETIQUETTE
Emily Holt, 1901

"We have not yet reached that stage of modernization where we follow our friends in procession to their last resting-places in taxicabs . . ."

THE CYCLOPAEDIA OF SOCIAL USAGE
Helen L. Roberts, 1913

"There are many funerals at which flowers are a burden,—there is such a profusion of them. Not only is it necessary to have a special coach to transport the huge floral emblems to the cemetery, but there they soon fade, leaving the wire forms to rust and become an eyesore until the caretaker of the section removes them. It is far better, if one does send flowers, to let them be bunches of loose blossoms, which may be strewn over the grave, and which, in fading, will not leave a hideous skeleton of stained wire to torture the sight of the first visitors to the newly-made grave."

EVERYDAY ETIQUETTE
Marion Harland and Virginia Van de Water, 1907

"No decent person laughs at a funeral . . ."

THE BAZAR BOOK OF DECORUM
Anonymous, 1870

FUNERAL FRILLS

Mourning clothing was an instant communication—before the days of the telephone and the telegraph—that a death had taken place. The black frock and parasol were both a warning and a haven, observes a writer: "A mourning dress does protect a woman while in deepest grief against the untimely gayety of a passing stranger. It is a wall, a cell of refuge. Behind a black veil she can hide herself as she goes out for business or recreation, fearless of any intrusion."

The style was not optional: "[I]t is deemed almost a sin for a woman to go into the street, to drive, or to walk, for two years, without a deep crape veil over her face," reports a Victorian author. This retreat in habiliment mirrored the mourner's retreat from life. For the first year she was neither to issue nor to accept invitations from society. Some authors protested this seclusion, concerned that it might provoke the very result it was intended to mourn: "There are some temperaments to whom this isolation long continued would prove fatal," worries a writer.

A morbid minority, however, seemed to relish the act of mourning, for they donned black at any opportunity, even for the demise of people whom

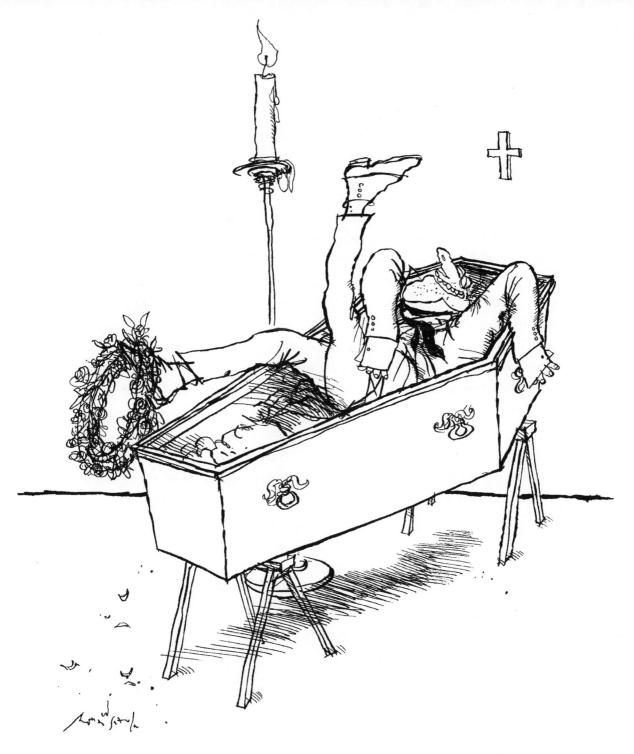

"*Avoid inquiring the state of mind of a departed friend, or relative, when paying a visit of condolence. This may cause mental distress to the survivors; for the deceased may have led an irregular life, and his death-bed may not have been so happy as could have been wished.*"

they had never met. "In America, with no fixity of rule," one writer reports, "ladies have been known to go into deepest mourning for their own relatives or those of their husbands, or for people, perhaps, whom they have never seen, and have remained as gloomy monuments of bereavement for seven or ten years, constantly in black. . . ."

But the professional mourner gave herself away by an inordinate attention to the image of grief. A sincere sorrower did not exhibit "an unseemly fear lest her bonnet will be unbecoming," nor did she discuss her mourning outfit with the same relish as she did her ball gown. "There is a ghoul-like ghastliness in talking about 'ornamental,' or 'becoming,' or 'complimentary' mourning," one author scolds. Another agrees: "[B]etter that a young widow should go out in scarlet and yellow on the day after her husband's funeral than wear weeds which attract attention on account of their flaunting bad taste and flippancy. One may not, one must not, one *can not* wear the very last cry of exaggerated fashion in crepe, nor may one be boisterous or flippant or sloppy in manner, without giving the impression to all beholders that one's spirit is posturing, tripping, or dancing on the grave of sacred memory."

"No one except a very tactless person would presume to ask of a friend in deep mourning for whom she was wearing it."

GOOD MANNERS FOR ALL OCCASIONS
Margaret E. Sangster, 1921

"Veils act as screens between ravaged faces and the eyes of passers-by."

VOGUE'S BOOK OF ETIQUETTE
The Editors of Vogue, 1923

"People with weak eyes or lungs must not wear a heavy crape veil over the face. It is loaded with arsenic, and is most dangerous to sight and breath."

MANNERS AND SOCIAL USAGES
Mrs. John Sherwood, 1897

"To attend a funeral in a flannel lounging-coat, checked trousers, gayly striped or dotted linen, a flaring necktie, brown shoes and a straw hat, is to demonstrate little self-respect and reverence for the solemn occasion."

ENCYCLOPAEDIA OF ETIQUETTE
Emily Holt, 1901

"Don't wear spats . . . at funerals."

McCALL'S BOOK OF EVERYDAY ETIQUETTE
Margaret Bevans with the Editors of McCall's *magazine, 1960*

"A widow still wearing her weeds, and at the same time carrying on an animated flirtation with some new admirer, is a sight to make the gods weep."

SOCIAL CUSTOMS
Florence Howe Hall, 1911

"Very little children in black are too pitiful."

ETIQUETTE
Emily Post, 1922

IN DEEPEST SYMPATHY

A mourner's missive was immediately recognized by the color of the sealing wax. Should the black wax be overlooked, the black-bordered stationery left no doubt as to the state of mind of the correspondent. Sometimes the mourner got carried away. "The autograph letter of condolence which Queen Victoria sent to Mrs. Lincoln when the President was assassinated was written on note-paper with a black border nearly an inch deep!" gossiped the etiquette writers. Such ostentation was in bad taste, they scolded: "No doubt all these things are proper enough in their way, but a narrow border of black tells the story of loss as well as an inch of coal-black gloom."

The black-border fashion was not limited to stationery. Some mourners adopted this look on their handkerchiefs, but gentlemen grievers abstained, heeding etiquette's rule: "No man of good taste carries a black-bordered handkerchief." Recalls an author: "The fashion of wearing handkerchiefs which are made with a two-inch square of white cambric and a four-inch border of black may well be deprecated. A gay young widow at Washington was once seen dancing at a reception, a few months after the death of her soldier husband, with a long black veil on, and holding in her black-gloved hand one of these handkerchiefs, which looked as if it had been dipped in ink. 'She should have dipped it in blood,' said a by-stander."

"Do not write long letters of condolence to those in affliction, or give them a sermon, advising them to bow to the will of Providence."

THE NEW CENTURY PERFECT SPEAKER
Edited by John Coulter, 1901

"To write a letter of congratulation on mourning paper is rather inconsistent."

TWENTIETH CENTURY ETIQUETTE
Annie Randall White, 1900

"Invitations should be sent to those in mourning the same as to other people, except during the first month of their bereavement when their grief is not intruded upon. The invitation will be declined of course, but it shows that they are not forgotten. Do not blunder, however, and send an invitation to the dead."

MODERN MANNERS AND SOCIAL FORMS
Julia M. Bradley, 1889

NOTES

INTRODUCTION

xi   *If anything:* Unattributed quotation, Anonymous, INQUIRE WITHIN FOR ANY-
THING YOU WANT TO KNOW (1858).

xii   *Never forget:* Anonymous, GEMS OF DEPORTMENT (1880).

xiii   *into the:* Ibid.

xiii   *People purchase:* The Right Hon. The Countess of *******, MIXING IN SOCIETY
(1869).

xiii   *All the:* C. E. Sargent, OUR HOME (1883).

xiii   *The woman:* Margaret Wade, SOCIAL USAGE IN AMERICA (1924).

xiii   *You ought:* Geneviève Antoine Dariaux, ACCENT ON ELEGANCE (1970).

xiii   *If everyone:* Giovanni Della Casa, GALATEO *OR* THE BOOK OF MANNERS (1558);
translated by R. S. Pine-Coffin (1958).

xiii   *Ladies should:* Emily Thornwell, THE LADY'S GUIDE TO COMPLETE ETIQUETTE
(1886).

xiii   *By all:* Alice-Leone Moats, NO NICE GIRL SWEARS (1933).

xiii   *Manners are:* Ibid.

xiv   *Books that:* Compiled by Mrs. H. O. Ward, SENSIBLE ETIQUETTE OF THE BEST SO-
CIETY (1878).

CHAPTER 1: MANNERS FOR LOVERS AND SPINSTERS

1   *Accepting presents:* Florence Hartley, THE LADIES' BOOK OF ETIQUETTE, AND MANUAL OF POLITENESS (1873).

1   *being of:* By a Woman of Fashion, ETIQUETTE FOR AMERICANS (1909).

1   *Many a:* Mrs. Annie R. White, POLITE SOCIETY AT HOME AND ABROAD (1891).

7   *likely to:* M. C. Dunbar, DUNBAR'S COMPLETE HANDBOOK OF ETIQUETTE (1884).

7   *Never lose:* Anonymous, INQUIRE WITHIN FOR ANYTHING YOU WANT TO KNOW (1858).

7   *though he:* Ibid.

7   *real or:* Paul E. Lowe, THE UP-TO-DATE UNIVERSAL LETTER WRITER (1912).

7   *Rejected suitors:* Richard A. Wells, MANNERS, CULTURE AND DRESS OF THE BEST AMERICAN SOCIETY (1890).

10 *herself to:* Margaret E. Sangster, GOOD MANNERS FOR ALL OCCASIONS (1921).

10 *She is:* Mrs. Humphry, ETIQUETTE FOR EVERY DAY (1904).

10 *Crying is:* Mrs. Humphry, MANNERS FOR WOMEN (1897).

10 *The bride:* Mrs. Humphry, ETIQUETTE FOR EVERY DAY (1904).

12 *The beginnings:* Margaret E. Sangster, GOOD MANNERS FOR ALL OCCASIONS (1921).

12 *Usually marriage:* Prof. B. G. Jefferis and J. L. Nichols, SEARCH LIGHTS ON HEALTH (1896).

12 *If the:* Dio Lewis, FIVE-MINUTE CHATS WITH YOUNG WOMEN, AND CERTAIN OTHER PARTIES (1874).

12 *[y]oung husbands:* Prof. B. G. Jefferis and J. L. Nichols, SEARCH LIGHTS ON HEALTH (1896).

12 *To be:* Ibid.

CHAPTER 2: MANNERS FOR BUTLERS AND SCULLERY MAIDS

15 *Why servants:* Lady Kitty Vincent, GOOD MANNERS (1924).

16 *Familiarity with:* Frances Stevens, THE USAGES OF THE BEST SOCIETY (1884).

16 *The days:* Lady Kitty Vincent, GOOD MANNERS (1924).

18 *To ring:* Julia M. Bradley, MODERN MANNERS AND SOCIAL FORMS (1889).

19 *To discuss:* Emily Holt, ENCYCLOPAEDIA OF ETIQUETTE (1901).

19 *If you:* S. A. Frost, FROST'S LAWS AND BY-LAWS OF AMERICAN SOCIETY (1869).

CHAPTER 3: MANNERS FOR GLUTTONS AND GASTRONOMES

23 *that is:* Julia M. Bradley, MODERN MANNERS AND SOCIAL FORMS (1889).

23   *is a:* Mrs. John Sherwood, MANNERS AND SOCIAL USAGES (1897).

23   *A person:* Anonymous, GEMS OF DEPORTMENT (1880).

23   *If such:* Miss Leslie, MISS LESLIE'S BEHAVIOUR BOOK (1859).

24   *It is:* Agnes H. Morton, ETIQUETTE (1892).

24   *that would:* Lillian Eichler, BOOK OF ETIQUETTE, vol. II (1921).

26   *the art:* Unattributed quotation, Cecil B. Hartley, THE GENTLEMEN'S BOOK OF ETIQUETTE AND MANUAL OF POLITENESS (1860).

26   *Awkwardness in:* Mrs. Hale, MANNERS: OR, HAPPY HOMES AND GOOD SOCIETY (1867).

26   *What more:* By One of Themselves, THE MANNERS OF THE ARISTOCRACY (18—).

28   *All the:* Mrs. Burton Kingsland, THE BOOK OF GOOD MANNERS (1901).

28   *each guest:* Mary Ronald, THE CENTURY COOK BOOK (1895).

28   *as devastated:* Geneviève Antoine Dariaux, ENTERTAINING WITH ELEGANCE (1965).

28   *Flowers should:* Florence Howe Hall, SOCIAL CUSTOMS (1911).

29   *It's possible:* Betty Allen and Mitchell Pirie Briggs, IF YOU PLEASE! (1942).

29   *A man:* Anonymous, THE LADIES' AND GENTLEMENS' LETTER-WRITER, AND GUIDE TO POLITE BEHAVIOR (ca. 1880).

30   *the crusade:* Anonymous, AS OTHERS SEE US (1890).

30   *but there:* Ibid.

30   *The knife:* Betty Allen and Mitchell Pirie Briggs, IF YOU PLEASE! (1942).

30   *upright on:* Mrs. E. B. Duffey, THE LADIES' AND GENTLEMEN'S ETIQUETTE (1877).

30   *When he:* William Gardiner, GETTING A FOOTHOLD (1927).

30   *You bring:* The Editors of *Esquire* magazine and Ron Butler, ESQUIRE'S GUIDE TO MODERN ETIQUETTE (1969).

30   *an added:* Anonymous, AS OTHERS SEE US (1890).

34   *[N]either etiquette:* Helen L. Roberts, THE CYCLOPAEDIA OF SOCIAL USAGE (1913).

34   *a tactless:* Ibid.

34   *I am:* Ibid.

34   *gallant elderly:* Frederick H. Martens, THE BOOK OF GOOD MANNERS (1923).

34   *dext'rously forth:* Translated by Francis Hawkins, YOUTHS BEHAVIOUR, OR DECENCY IN CONVERSATION AMONGST MEN (1663); edited by Charles Moore, GEORGE WASHINGTON'S RULES OF CIVILITY AND DECENT BEHAVIOUR IN COMPANY AND CONVERSATION (1747; 1926).

34   *never use:* Betty Allen and Mitchell Pirie Briggs, IF YOU PLEASE! (1942).

34   *sometimes be:* Mrs. F. L. Gillette and Hugo Ziemann, THE WHITE HOUSE COOK BOOK (1890).

39 quatorzième, *or:* Anonymous, THE BAZAR BOOK OF DECORUM (1870).

39 *order and:* M. C. Dunbar, DUNBAR'S COMPLETE HANDBOOK OF ETIQUETTE (1884).

39 *But don't:* Ibid.

39 *for all:* Ibid.

39 *let flow:* Ibid.

39 *this often:* S. A. Frost, FROST'S LAWS AND BY-LAWS OF AMERICAN SOCIETY (1869).

39 *gentlemen left:* Helen L. Roberts, THE CYCLOPAEDIA OF SOCIAL USAGE (1913).

43 *[H]owever strong:* Francis W. Crowninshield, MANNERS FOR THE METROPOLIS (1909).

CHAPTER 4: MANNERS FOR WALTZERS AND WALLFLOWERS

45 *Nothing better:* Julia M. Bradley, MODERN MANNERS AND SOCIAL FORMS (1889).

45 *Good taste:* Anonymous, THE MANNERS THAT WIN (1880).

45 *Unexceptionable:* Ibid.

45 *neither too:* Abby Buchanan Longstreet, SOCIAL ETIQUETTE OF NEW YORK (1887).

45 *Autograph visiting:* S. A. Frost, FROST'S LAWS AND BY-LAWS OF AMERICAN SOCIETY (1869).

45 *a vulgarism:* Ibid.

46 *[W]ith the:* Florence Howe Hall, SOCIAL CUSTOMS (1911).

46 *A good:* Anonymous, THE STANDARD CYCLOPAEDIA OF USEFUL KNOWLEDGE, vol. V (1896).

50 *At a:* Francis W. Crowninshield, MANNERS FOR THE METROPOLIS (1909).

50 *The guest:* Edited by Lily Haxworth Wallace, THE NEW AMERICAN ETIQUETTE (1941).

50 *[P]lease, if:* Geneviève Antoine Dariaux, ELEGANCE (1964).

50 *Poodles are:* Miss Leslie, MISS LESLIE'S BEHAVIOUR BOOK (1859).

50 *Dogs have:* Mrs. Annie R. White, POLITE SOCIETY AT HOME AND ABROAD (1891).

50 *Besides, your:* M. C. Dunbar, DUNBAR'S COMPLETE HANDBOOK OF ETIQUETTE (1884).

51 *is the:* Anonymous, THE HABITS OF GOOD SOCIETY (1859).

52 *loses his:* Annie Randall White, TWENTIETH CENTURY ETIQUETTE (1900).

52 *Few are:* J. H. Kellogg, PLAIN FACTS FOR OLD AND YOUNG (1879).

52 *[w]hen acquired:* Ibid.

55 *The pleasure:* Maud C. Cooke, SOCIAL ETIQUETTE (18—).

56 *indiscriminately:* Compiled by John H. Young, OUR DEPORTMENT (1881).

56 *Ladies never:* Anonymous, THE STANDARD CYCLOPAEDIA OF USEFUL KNOWLEDGE, vol. V (1896).

56 *a limp:* Edited by Albert Ellery Berg, THE UNIVERSAL SELF-INSTRUCTOR (1882).

56 *[B]y all:* Eleanor Roosevelt, ELEANOR ROOSEVELT'S BOOK OF COMMON SENSE ETIQUETTE (1962).

56 *the melancholy:* Anonymous, THE HABITS OF GOOD SOCIETY (1859).

56 *shaken violently:* Emily Post, ETIQUETTE (1922).

56 *[T]he worst:* Anonymous, AS OTHERS SEE US (1890).

59 *Many accomplishments:* Mrs. Annie R. White, POLITE SOCIETY AT HOME AND ABROAD (1891).

59 *mentally appreciative:* Virginia Van de Water, PRESENT DAY ETIQUETTE (1936).

59 *Many young:* Florence Howe Hall, SOCIAL CUSTOMS (1911).

59 *I don't:* Lord Chesterfield, THE AMERICAN CHESTERFIELD (18—).

59 *[A] performance:* Casimir Bohn, BOHN'S MANUAL OF ETIQUETTE IN WASHINGTON (1856).

60 *resulted in:* Marion Harland and Virginia Van de Water, EVERYDAY ETIQUETTE (1907).

60 *A husband:* Pye Henry Chavasse, WOMAN AS A WIFE AND MOTHER (1870).

60 *A man:* Ibid.

63 *[T]he well-bred:* Anonymous, THE HABITS OF GOOD SOCIETY (1859).

63 *odious and:* Florence Howe Hall, SOCIAL CUSTOMS (1911).

63 *It is:* Florence Howe Hall, THE CORRECT THING IN GOOD SOCIETY (1902).

63 *earnestly advised:* M. C. Dunbar, DUNBAR'S COMPLETE HANDBOOK OF ETIQUETTE (1884).

63 *Loud strains:* Margaret Watts Livingston, et al., CORRECT SOCIAL USAGE, vol. II (1906).

63 *sacred:* Anonymous, THE STANDARD BOOK ON POLITENESS, GOOD BEHAVIOR AND SOCIAL ETIQUETTE (1884).

63 *the utmost:* Ibid.

63 *in order:* M. C. Dunbar, DUNBAR'S COMPLETE HANDBOOK OF ETIQUETTE (1884).

63 *An introduction:* Anonymous, THE STANDARD CYCLOPAEDIA OF USEFUL KNOWLEDGE, vol. V (1896).

CHAPTER 5: MANNERS FOR PREENERS AND DANDIES

69 *A man's:* Mrs. Humphry, MANNERS FOR MEN (1897).

69 *is the:* Casimir Bohn, BOHN'S MANUAL OF ETIQUETTE IN WASHINGTON (1856).

69 *It is:* Charles William Day, HINTS ON ETIQUETTE (1843).

69 *The best:* Prof. B. G. Jefferis and J. L. Nichols, SEARCH LIGHTS ON HEALTH (1896).

70 *There is:* Anonymous, THE HABITS OF GOOD SOCIETY (1859).

70 *the slouchy:* Prof. B. G. Jefferis and J. L. Nichols, SEARCH LIGHTS ON HEALTH (1896).

70 *A gentleman:* Compiled by Nugent Robinson, COLLIER'S CYCLOPEDIA OF COMMERCIAL AND SOCIAL INFORMATION (1882).

72 *Most of:* Margery Wilson, THE NEW ETIQUETTE (1940).

72 *It is:* Geneviève Antoine Dariaux, ACCENT ON ELEGANCE (1970).

72 *Women seldom:* Thos. E. Hill, HILL'S MANUAL OF SOCIAL AND BUSINESS FORMS (1882).

72 *may be:* Anonymous, DECORUM (1877).

72 *so that:* Dio Lewis, FIVE-MINUTE CHATS WITH YOUNG WOMEN, AND CERTAIN OTHER PARTIES (1874).

74 *Let your:* John Ashton, MEN MAIDENS AND MANNERS A HUNDRED YEARS AGO (1888).

74 *Shampooing is:* Annie Randall White, TWENTIETH CENTURY ETIQUETTE (1900).

74 *New England:* Mrs. Child, THE AMERICAN FRUGAL HOUSEWIFE (1832).

74 *Good health:* Alex M. Gow, GOOD MORALS AND GENTLE MANNERS (1873).

75 *Put the:* A. Lyman Phillips, A BACHELOR'S CUPBOARD (1906).

76 *However ugly:* Richard A. Wells, MANNERS, CULTURE AND DRESS OF THE BEST AMERICAN SOCIETY (1890).

76 *We have:* Anonymous, THE LADY'S BOOK OF MANNERS (1870).

76 *If emerald:* Emily Post, ETIQUETTE (1922).

76 *Remember the:* Enid A. Haupt, THE SEVENTEEN BOOK OF YOUNG LIVING (1957).

78 *Fat women:* Emily Post, ETIQUETTE (1922).

78 *Frills, and:* Anonymous, ETIQUETTE FOR THE LADIES (1849).

78 *women with:* Mary D. Chambers, TEENS AND TWENTIES (1923).

80 *In the:* Margaret E. Sangster, GOOD MANNERS FOR ALL OCCASIONS (1921).

80 *Flirting a:* Anonymous, THE MANNERS THAT WIN (1880).

80 *When seated:* Florence Hartley, THE LADIES' BOOK OF ETIQUETTE, AND MANUAL OF POLITENESS (1873).

83 *A beautiful:* Mrs. Annie R. White, POLITE SOCIETY AT HOME AND ABROAD (1891).

83 *There is:* Anonymous, AS OTHERS SEE US (1890).

83 *Large mittens:* Mrs. Annie R. White, POLITE SOCIETY AT HOME AND ABROAD (1891).

83 *Many a:* Anonymous, DECORUM (1877).

83 *The Early:* Mary D. Chambers, TEENS AND TWENTIES (1923).

83 *A bottle:* Laura C. Holloway, THE HEARTHSTONE: OR, LIFE AT HOME (1883).

84 *I knew:* Anonymous, AS OTHERS SEE US (1890).

CHAPTER 6: MANNERS FOR WITS AND RACONTEURS

87 *A woman:* By One of Themselves, THE MANNERS OF THE ARISTOCRACY (18—).

87 *It is:* Unattributed quotation, Mrs. Burton Kingsland, THE BOOK OF GOOD MANNERS (1901).

87 *All topics:* Anonymous, GOOD MANNERS (1870).

87 *Ladies abhor:* M. C. Dunbar, DUNBAR'S COMPLETE HANDBOOK OF ETIQUETTE (1884).

87 *[A]greeability, rather:* Henry Lunettes, THE AMERICAN GENTLEMAN'S GUIDE TO POLITENESS AND FASHION (1863).

87 *Never ask:* Arthur Martine, MARTINE'S HAND-BOOK OF ETIQUETTE (1866).

87 *As a:* Henry Lunettes, THE AMERICAN GENTLEMAN'S GUIDE TO POLITENESS AND FASHION (1863).

87 *Some authorities:* Compiled by John H. Young, OUR DEPORTMENT (1881).

88 *show violent:* K. H. and M. B. H., 100 POINTS IN ETIQUETTE AND 101 DON'TS (1929).

90 *A man:* By a Gentleman, THE PERFECT GENTLEMAN (1860).

90 *"arise" and:* The Editors of *Vogue*, VOGUE'S BOOK OF ETIQUETTE (1924).

90 *If they:* By a Gentleman, THE PERFECT GENTLEMAN (1860).

92 *The well-bred:* The Editors of *Vogue*, VOGUE'S BOOK OF ETIQUETTE (1924).

92 *[D]o not:* Emily Post, ETIQUETTE (1950).

92 *Slang is:* Laura Thornborough, ETIQUETTE FOR EVERYBODY (1923).

92 *[D]umbunny not:* Ethel Frey Cushing, CULTURE AND GOOD MANNERS (1926).

92 *If men:* Mrs. Annie R. White, POLITE SOCIETY AT HOME AND ABROAD (1891).

92 *The women:* Julia M. Bradley, MODERN MANNERS AND SOCIAL FORMS (1889).

92 *Avoid an:* Mrs. E. B. Duffey, THE LADIES' AND GENTLEMEN'S ETIQUETTE (1877).

92 *The young:* J. H. Kellogg, PLAIN FACTS FOR OLD AND YOUNG (1879).

97 *It is:* Mrs. Annie R. White, POLITE SOCIETY AT HOME AND ABROAD (1891).

97   *you can:* Geneviève Antoine Dariaux, ACCENT ON ELEGANCE (1970).

97   *[T]hese famous:* Ibid.

99   *To laugh:* Helen Ekin Starrett, THE CHARM OF FINE MANNERS (1920).

99   *The ruder:* Alex M. Gow, GOOD MORALS AND GENTLE MANNERS (1873).

99   *In my:* The Earl of Chesterfield, LETTERS TO HIS SON (1748; 1937).

99   *There is:* Mrs. Humphry, MANNERS FOR WOMEN (1897).

CHAPTER 7: MANNERS FOR HOSTS AND HOUSEGUESTS

103   *When showing:* Viola Tree, CAN I HELP YOU? (1937).

103   *Avoid, in:* Ibid.

104   *chosen more:* Emily Post, ETIQUETTE (1922).

104   PLEASE FILL: Emily Post, ETIQUETTE (1942).

106   *If you:* Emily Post, ETIQUETTE (1922).

106   *Light all:* Viola Tree, CAN I HELP YOU? (1937).

110   *People of:* Lillian Eichler, THE NEW BOOK OF ETIQUETTE, vol. II (1924).

110   *questionable whether:* Censor, DON'T (1888).

111   *The lesser:* Mrs. L. H. Sigourney, LETTERS TO YOUNG LADIES (1836).

111   *has been:* Edited by Henry W. Ruoff, THE CENTURY BOOK OF FACTS (1908).

111   *It looks:* Julia M. Bradley, MODERN MANNERS AND SOCIAL FORMS (1889).

111   *[W]e must:* Emily Thornwell, THE LADY'S GUIDE TO COMPLETE ETIQUETTE (1886).

111   *In a:* Maud C. Cooke, SOCIAL ETIQUETTE (18—).

111   *irretrievably glued:* Mrs. John Sherwood, MANNERS AND SOCIAL USAGES (1897).

117   *A glance:* Compiled by Mrs. H. O. Ward, SENSIBLE ETIQUETTE OF THE BEST SO-
CIETY (1878).

117   *Novel-reading:* J. H. Kellogg, PLAIN FACTS FOR OLD AND YOUNG (1879).

117   *The result:* Prof. A. E. Willis, HUMAN NATURE (1907).

117   *We will:* Anonymous, THE LADY'S BOOK OF MANNERS (1870).

117   *the reading:* Ibid.

117   *A confirmed:* J. H. Kellogg, *Plain Facts for Old and Young* (1879).

120   *[u]nless you:* Anonymous, *Etiquette for Gentlemen* (1925).

121   *gypsying by:* Anonymous, THE MANNERS THAT WIN (1880).

121   *[N]othing is:* Anonymous, THE HABITS OF GOOD SOCIETY (1859).

121   *Gentlemen at:* S. A. Frost, FROST'S LAWS AND BY-LAWS OF AMERICAN SOCIETY
(1869).

121   *it is:* By One of Themselves, THE MANNERS OF THE ARISTOCRACY (18—).

121   *One does:* Anonymous, THE SUCCESSFUL HOUSEKEEPER (1882).

121   *Care should:* By One of Themselves, THE MANNERS OF THE ARISTOCRACY (18—).

121   *resume their:* Eliza Cheadle, MANNERS OF MODERN SOCIETY (187-).

121   *If only:* Anonymous, ETIQUETTE FOR GENTLEMEN (1925).

121   *It is:* Lady Kitty Vincent, GOOD MANNERS (1924).

122   *If you:* Mary Lou Munson, PRACTICAL ETIQUETTE FOR THE MODERN MAN (1964).

122   *[t]he party:* Anonymous, ETIQUETTE FOR GENTLEMEN (1925).

122   *a good:* By A Member of the Aristocracy, MANNERS AND RULES OF GOOD SOCIETY (1901).

122   *a good:* Ibid.

122   *And never:* Anonymous, ETIQUETTE FOR LADIES (1925).

124   *no matter:* Florence Howe Hall, SOCIAL CUSTOMS (1911).

126   *Very gallant:* Maud C. Cooke, SOCIAL ETIQUETTE (18—).

126   *The "uneducated":* Alex M. Gow, GOOD MORALS AND GENTLE MANNERS (1873).

126   *that will:* Maud C. Cooke, SOCIAL ETIQUETTE (18—).

126   *A lady:* Annie Randall White, TWENTIETH CENTURY ETIQUETTE (1900).

128   *may be:* Rev. C. W. de Lyon Nichols, et al., CORRECT SOCIAL USAGE, vol. I (1906).

128   *The newly:* Ibid.

128   *Our most:* J. H. Kellogg, PLAIN FACTS FOR OLD AND YOUNG (1879).

CHAPTER 8: MANNERS FOR COMMUTERS AND CLERKS

133   *As a:* Agnes H. Morton, ETIQUETTE (1892).

133   *[a]s a:* Ibid.

133   *a young:* Florence Howe Hall, SOCIAL CUSTOMS (1911).

133   *[n]o young:* Emily Post, ETIQUETTE (1922).

134   *The youth:* Laura Thornborough, ETIQUETTE FOR EVERYBODY (1923).

134   *that the:* Frances Angell, COMPETE! (1935).

138   *The power:* Anonymous, GOOD MANNERS (1870).

138   *may come:* Ibid.

138   *Never assail:* Anonymous, THE HABITS OF GOOD SOCIETY (1859).

138   *an important:* Ibid.

146   *Should you:* Count Alfred D'Orsay, ETIQUETTE; OR, A GUIDE TO THE USAGES OF SOCIETY (1843).

148   *The best:* Mrs. Burton Kingsland, THE BOOK OF GOOD MANNERS (1901).

148   *an unseeing:* Ibid.

148   *Mrs. Brown:* Anonymous, GOOD MANNERS (1870).

148   *Most people:* S. A. Frost, FROST'S LAWS AND BY-LAWS OF AMERICAN SOCIETY (1869).

CHAPTER 9: MANNERS FOR TOURISTS AND TRAVELERS

151   *The rage:* Florence Howe Hall, SOCIAL CUSTOMS (1911).

151   *And with:* Marion Harland and Virginia Van de Water, EVERYDAY ETIQUETTE (1907).

151   *The wealthy:* Helen L. Roberts, THE CYCLOPAEDIA OF SOCIAL USAGE (1913).

152   *[t]o sulk:* Ibid.

154   *One of:* Frances Angell, COMPETE! (1935).

154   *The best:* Anonymous, THE SUCCESSFUL HOUSEKEEPER (1882).

154   *Spit in:* Julia M. Bradley, MODERN MANNERS AND SOCIAL FORMS (1889).

154   *At any:* Emily Holt, ENCYCLOPAEDIA OF ETIQUETTE (1901).

154   *A horse:* Laura C. Holloway, THE HEARTHSTONE; OR, LIFE AT HOME (1883).

154   *Here is:* Edited by E. Gretchen VanderMeer, POTPOURRI OF YESTERYEAR (1974).

157   *Do not:* Anonymous, ETIQUETTE FOR GENTLEMEN (1925).

157   *Because of:* Ethel Frey Cushing, CULTURE AND GOOD MANNERS (1926).

157   *It is:* Florence Howe Hall, THE CORRECT THING IN GOOD SOCIETY (1902).

158   *[R]emember that:* Ibid.

158   *Only a:* Anonymous, THE BOOK OF BUSINESS ETIQUETTE (1922).

162   *There is:* S. A. Frost, FROST'S LAWS AND BY-LAWS OF AMERICAN SOCIETY (1869).

162   *No lady:* Ibid.

162   *No lady:* Ibid.

162   *To avoid:* Anonymous, THE MANNERS THAT WIN (1880).

162   *Ladies know:* Mme. Celnart, THE GENTLEMAN AND LADY'S BOOK OF POLITENESS (1835).

CHAPTER 10: MANNERS FOR TOMBOYS AND SISSIES

165   *[H]omes are:* Margaret E. Sangster, GOOD MANNERS FOR ALL OCCASIONS (1921).

165   *spin them:* Moses Folsom and J. D. O'Connor, TREASURES OF SCIENCE, HISTORY AND LITERATURE (1879).

165   *no light:* Anonymous, AS OTHERS SEE US (1890).

166 *is expected:* Ibid.

166   *The days:* Emily Post, ETIQUETTE (1922).

CHAPTER 11: MANNERS FOR CORPSES AND WIDOWS

171 *The human:* Anonymous, THE BAZAR BOOK OF DECORUM (1870).

171 *virginal robes:* Margaret E. Sangster, GOOD MANNERS FOR ALL OCCASIONS (1921).

171 *For women:* Mrs. Burton Kingsland, THE BOOK OF GOOD MANNERS (1901).

171 *It is:* Florence Howe Hall, SOCIAL CUSTOMS (1911).

171 *Courtesy is:* Horace J. Gardner and Patricia Farren, COURTESY BOOK (1937).

174 *At funerals:* Margery Wilson, CHARM (1934).

174 *If you:* Ibid.

174 *[e]arth is:* Laura Thornborough, ETIQUETTE FOR EVERYBODY (1923).

174 *Flowers on:* Compiled by Mrs. H. O. Ward, SENSIBLE ETIQUETTE OF THE BEST SOCIETY (1878).

175 *[E]tiquette unites:* Lillian Eichler, BOOK OF ETIQUETTE, vol. I (1921).

176 *A mourning:* Mrs. John Sherwood, MANNERS AND SOCIAL USAGES (1897).

176 *[I]t is:* Ibid.

176 *There are:* Annie Randall White, TWENTIETH CENTURY ETIQUETTE (1900).

178 *In America:* Mrs. John Sherwood, MANNERS AND SOCIAL USAGES (1897).

178 *an unseemly:* Annie Randall White, TWENTIETH CENTURY ETIQUETTE (1900).

178 *There is:* Mrs. John Sherwood, MANNERS AND SOCIAL USAGES (1897).

178 *[B]etter that:* Emily Post, ETIQUETTE (1922).

179 *The autograph:* Florence Howe Hall, SOCIAL CUSTOMS (1911).

179 *No doubt:* Mrs. John Sherwood, MANNERS AND SOCIAL USAGES (1897).

180 *No man:* Lillian Eichler, THE NEW BOOK OF ETIQUETTE, vol. II (1924).

180 *The fashion:* Mrs. John Sherwood, MANNERS AND SOCIAL USAGES (1897).

The manner of others toward us
is usually the reflex of our manner toward them.
As men have howled into the wood
so it has ever howled out.

THE MENTOR
Alfred Ayres, 1884